A READING OF

Paradise Lost

Oxford University Press, Ely House, London W. 1

GLASGOW NEW YORK TORONTO MELBOURNE WELLINGTON
CAPE TOWN SALISBURY IBADAN NAIROBI LUSAKA ADDIS ABABA
BOMBAY CALCUTTA MADRAS KARACHI LAHORE DACCA
KUALA LUMPUR HONG KONG TOKYO

A READING OF
Paradise Lost

BY

HELEN GARDNER

━━━━

THE ALEXANDER LECTURES

IN THE

UNIVERSITY OF TORONTO

1962

OXFORD
AT THE CLARENDON PRESS

REPRINTED LITHOGRAPHICALLY IN GREAT BRITAIN
(WITH CORRECTIONS)
1967

TO
HERBERT AND EMILY
DAVIS

PREFACE

WHEN the University of Toronto honoured me in 1960 by inviting me to deliver the Alexander Lectures in 1962 I was planning to write a short book on *Paradise Lost*. Although it seemed rash to offer lectures on this subject in a university famous for its contribution to Miltonic studies, it seemed cowardly to refrain from lecturing on a subject that was much occupying my mind and to hunt round instead for some safer topic. But I had no sooner committed myself than I realized that I was by no means alone in feeling an urge to write on '*Paradise Lost* Today' and that something like a spate of books was appearing or was announced on Milton's Epic. To mention only a few of the most outstanding, J. B. Broadbent's *Some Graver Subject* and John Peter's *A Critique of 'Paradise Lost'* appeared in 1960, and in the same year Professor Frank Kermode edited a volume of essays on *The Living Milton*. In 1961 Professor Gerald Wilkes joined in from Sydney with *The Thesis of 'Paradise Lost'*, a rejoinder to Sydney's most famous contribution to the subject, the late Professor Waldock's *'Paradise Lost' and its Critics* (1947), which was republished in the same year as a paperback. At the end of the year there appeared Professor Empson's *Milton's God*, the first sustained attempt to overthrow what had become the orthodox academic view of the poem, that expounded by Charles Williams, followed by C. S. Lewis in his immensely influential *A Preface to 'Paradise Lost'* (1942), and by Professor Douglas Bush in *'Paradise Lost' in Our Time* (1945). All these were available to me as I sat down to compose my lectures, and I was aware that Professor Bernard Wright's long-awaited study was in the press and that Professor Joseph Summers was finishing a book on *Paradise*

Lost. Both Professor Wright's *Milton's 'Paradise Lost'* and Professor Summers's *The Muse's Method* appeared in 1962, as well as Professor Jackson Cope's *The Metaphoric Structure of 'Paradise Lost'*. In 1963 Mr. Christopher Ricks produced *Milton's Grand Style*, an attempt at a full rebuttal of Dr. Leavis's strictures on Milton's language, and Mrs. Ferry in *Milton's Epic Voice* discussed and analysed Milton's technique of presentation. I can hardly claim that these lectures were on a neglected masterpiece.

All the same, the number of books that have appeared and are appearing, not to mention innumerable articles, bear witness to the difficulty that the twentieth century finds in coming to terms with this mighty monument of faith, courage, and art. It was my own experience of this difficulty on a small scale, in teaching and lecturing on *Paradise Lost* to first-year undergraduates, that made me want to analyse and justify my own belief in the permanent greatness of Milton's greatest poem. I had another reason. Since my schooldays I have loved and enjoyed the poetry of both Donne and Milton, and never felt any wish to exalt the one at the expense of the other. Having been engaged on and off for the last fifteen years in editing the poetry of Donne I thought it would be refreshing to turn to write on *Paradise Lost*, not as Miltonist *pur sang* but as a reader who approaches the poem with knowledge of its age gained from editing and annotating a very different kind of poetry. With both Donne and Milton a modern critic has to steer a course between two extremes: the attempt to interpret their poetry solely in the terms of their own age, and the attempt to interpret it solely in the terms of ours. The pendulum of taste has swung very markedly in the last few years, and Donne is looked at very much more coolly than when I was young. But the attempt to reduce him to nothing more than the 'Monarch of Wit' ignores those qualities in him which made it possible for men and women three hundred years after his death to find

in him a language of feeling appropriate to the needs of
their hearts and minds. The same problem arises with
Paradise Lost.

I have never felt happy at the attempt to confine the
meaning of *Paradise Lost* to the meaning that it had for
its own century, even if this were discoverable with cer-
tainty, which I doubt. I have never been able to dismiss
the reading of the poem by two men of genius, with much
in common with Milton in their 'Prophetic strain', Blake
and Shelley. The fact that most readers of the poem who
approach it without the aid of scholarship concur in finding its main imaginative appeal in the figure of Satan has
always seemed to me a fact that criticism of the poem must
come to terms with. It is not enough to demonstrate by
argument that 'the Devil is an Ass' if the common reader
so obstinately persists in regarding him as heroic. Many
years ago I tried to find a way of reconciling the historical–
theological interpretation with the subjective in an essay
on the character and role of Satan that I am reprinting in
this volume. I print it as it was published, with a note of
reservation that I would now make. My present position
as expressed in the lectures has developed from the views
expressed in 1948. I have added also a short paper on
the first illustrations to *Paradise Lost,* published in 1956,
which suggests that even in Milton's own century Satan,
unlike the other characters of the epic, could not be re-
duced to a type.

I have to thank the publishers (John Murray, and Holt,
Rinehart, and Winston, Inc.) and Sir Kenneth Clark for
permission to quote from *Looking at Pictures* (1960), and
the Victoria and Albert Museum, for allowing me to re-
produce Raphael's Cartoon of *The Miraculous Draught of
Fishes.* I have also to thank the Warburg Institute which
many years ago photographed Medina's illustrations to
Paradise Lost for me from my own copy of the edition of
1692.

Quotations from *Paradise Lost* are taken from H. C. Beeching's text, formerly in the Oxford Standard Authors edition of *Milton's Poetical Works*. While this book was going through the press, Professor Empson published a revised and enlarged edition of *Milton's God*, too late for me to modify references to the first edition of his book.

It remains for me to thank most warmly all those at the University of Toronto who invited me and made my stay while delivering these lectures so delightful. It is a grief to me that while this book was in preparation Professor A. S. P. Woodhouse died and I cannot thank him for all his kindness as my host, for his graciousness in taking the Chair, and for the exemplary patience he showed in listening to a trespasser on the field he had made so much his own.

HELEN GARDNER

CONTENTS

PLATES

I

PARADISE LOST TODAY

THE attack on the poetical style of *Paradise Lost* and on Milton as a deformer of the English language, exercising a malign influence on those poets who came beneath his sway, is now a part of literary history. The issue is dead. I say this in spite of the fact that recently Mr. Christopher Ricks has attempted to combat T. S. Eliot and Dr. Leavis on their own ground by displaying the sensitiveness and subtlety of Milton's epic style and its capacity to endure and repay close verbal criticism.[1] But though he is on the whole successful in challenging them in detail he pays almost no attention to what was the fundamental ground of complaint: that Milton's epic style is highly artificial, that his syntax is very far from the syntax of common speech, that his idiom is 'foreign'. To put it crudely, it is impossible to read *Paradise Lost* aloud without going far beyond the range of one's normal mode of speech. It is, on the other hand, perfectly possible to speak the verse of Shakespeare as if it were prose, and many of our most celebrated actors are praised for doing so. I would not wish to suggest that I approve of this practice. I only wish to make the point that what can be done, although with great loss, with Shakespeare could not even be attempted with *Paradise Lost*. The late Professor C. S. Lewis put an end to argument on this main issue when he conceded the accuracy of Dr. Leavis's analysis of the 'properties of Milton's epic verse', but added: 'It is not that he and I see different things when we look at *Paradise Lost*. He sees and hates

[1] C. Ricks, *Milton's Grand Style*, 1963.

the very same that I see and love.'[1] The attack on Milton
as a bad influence on subsequent poets was the most
curious of the charges against him, for surely no English
poet has had a worse influence than Shakespeare, whom
the anti-Miltonists idolized. Eliot himself made this point
in his British Academy lecture of 1947 when he conceded
that 'one might argue that *King Stephen* was more blighted
by Shakespeare than *Hyperion* by Milton'.[2] He could
have added that it is hardly possible to regard Chaucer
as a good influence on the English Chaucerians of the
fifteenth century, and that the Spenserians are not the most
lively poets of the seventeenth century. What Dryden,
speaking more truly than he intended, said of Shakespeare
could be applied to many of our greatest and most individual poets:

> But Shakespeare's magic could not copied be;
> Within that circle none durst walk but he.[3]

From the great poets lesser men have only caught the
superficialities of style. At least we may say of Milton
that imitation of *Paradise Lost* inspired one poem, *Hyperion*, which if it is to be called a failure, is a failure
so glorious that it calls into question what we mean by
success; and that the greatest of his 'sons' was inspired
by *Paradise Lost* to speak 'On Man, on Nature, and on

---

[1] *A Preface to 'Paradise Lost'*, 1942, p. 130. The essay by Dr. Leavis that is
referred to appeared in *Scrutiny* in 1933 and was republished in *Revaluation*,
1936, in the same year as Eliot published his 'A Note on the Verse of John Milton'
in *Essays and Studies* (1935). Eliot had, of course, been attacking Milton on the
same lines for many years, as had Mr. Ezra Pound; see, for instance, the celebrated essay on 'The Metaphysical Poets' of 1921.

[2] That Eliot's own 'Chinese Wall' was much more the blank verse of Shakespeare than the blank verse of Milton is suggested in my discussion of his efforts
to find his own 'voice' in the first chapter of my *The Art of T. S. Eliot*, 1949,
pp. 1–34.

[3] 'Prologue to *The Tempest*.' Dryden is merely apologizing for Shakespeare's
having 'writ as people then believed', his own age having outgrown belief in
'magic'; but the lines always come to my mind when I read post-Shakespearian
dramatic verse.

Human Life' in a voice that matches Milton's grave, impassioned, and eloquent tone but is all his own. Wordsworth is Milton's greatest 'son' as Milton is Spenser's, and if we are to attempt to assess Milton's influence we must take into account *The Prelude* as well as *Hyperion*.

The rejection of Milton as our great master of the 'artificial style' can now be seen as an inevitable accompaniment of the poetic achievement of the first half of the twentieth century, and it has died with the death of the poetic movement that caused it. By one of the ironies of literary history, recent critics, notably Mr. Graham Hough,[1] now describe the movement led by Mr. Pound and Eliot as an aberration and see them not as writing in the recovered true tradition of English poetry, as they saw themselves, but as following a lone trail that led to a dead end. I do not accept this view; but as neither Mr. Hough nor I can be proved right before we have both been many years in the grave, it would be a waste of time and energy for us to argue the point. I must, however, agree that Pound and Eliot are no longer important influences on young writers. It is indeed difficult to see anything that can be regarded as a literary movement at the moment. There is none of that sense of purpose and confidence in achievement that makes poets in the pride of their own mastery and the consciousness of the value of their own ideals reverse the values of the past and denigrate what their fathers admired. Although no poet writing today has a comparable ideal, the absence of any strong poetic movement has made possible a renewed appreciation of the ideal of 'magnificence' as a legitimate poetic ideal. A sensitive and distinguished lyric poet, Professor Frank Prince, has opened the door to a fresh approach to Milton's versification with his brief but packed book on *The Italian Element in Milton's Verse*, published in 1954, and Mr. John Wain, also a very

[1] See *Image and Experience*, 1960.

un-Miltonic poet, has confessed himself an enthusiast for Milton[1] and drawn a suggestive parallel between Milton and Yeats, whose poetry seems more congenial to the poets of this decade than the poetry of Eliot. Although the argument over Milton's style lingers in universities, it does not seem to me to be relevant to the linguistic and poetic concerns of today.

But if the argument over Milton's style is now a thing of the past, having like most such arguments much increased our understanding of the topic disputed, the argument over his choice of subject, conduct of the narrative, and success in his avowed purpose is still very much alive, and took an interesting new turn with Professor Empson's *Milton's God*, published in 1961. The question of what *Paradise Lost* has to offer to a modern reader, Christian or non-Christian, is a central critical issue, on which two views are sharply opposed. The question of what a poem offers to us is the central critical question with all great works of past ages. It obtrudes itself particularly pressingly with *Paradise Lost* because of Milton's intense belief that he was writing a poem that should be 'doctrinal to a nation' and his desire to be 'an interpreter of the best and sagest things'. His claim to instruct is overt and cannot be ignored. In addition, the Christian scheme of redemption which he set himself to illuminate for our imaginations is not a dead system that can be regarded with historical detachment. It still lives to be accepted or rejected by the mind and conscience today. *Paradise Lost* has to speak to those who find the basic tenets of Christianity intellectually untenable and its moral teaching repugnant, and also to those who feel that the theological concerns of the seventeenth century are grotesquely remote from the religious thought and experience of today and that Milton's stress and emphasis is unacceptable.

[1] See 'Strength and Isolation', an essay contributed to *The Living Milton*, edited by Frank Kermode, 1960.

That Milton showed extraordinary temerity in taking for his subject the 'vast Design' of the Christian myth as it had developed through seventeen centuries was recognized from the beginning, and Marvell's verses, added in the second edition of *Paradise Lost*, may be regarded as addressed to the Christian reader aghast at the poet's boldness in attempting to cast this hallowed story into the form of a classical epic. But Marvell confesses that his doubts, on reading 'the Argument', that the poet

> would ruine (for I saw him strong)
> The sacred Truths to Fable and old Song,

were quieted as he read the poem itself by a 'Majesty' reigning through the work which

> Draws the Devout, deterring the Profane.

He praises Milton's 'gravity' (*gravitas*, or weight) and his 'ease' (*facilitas*, fluency and grace) that inspire in us 'delight and horrour', the 'Plume so strong, so equal, and so soft' on which he soars 'above humane flight', and declares that his verse is like his 'Theme sublime'.

It does not appear that Marvell, whose sensibility has proved so congenial to twentieth-century readers, was in any way offended by *Paradise Lost*; and Dryden's complaint against Milton's subject was not on the grounds of its unsuitability for extended narrative treatment in the form of a classical epic, but on grounds of epic precedent. The subject of an epic had always been an enterprise successfully performed by the hero, and Milton had chosen a subject in which the Devil was successful and therefore must be regarded as playing the traditional hero's role: the 'giant' has 'foiled the knight, and driven him out of his stronghold, to wander through the world with his lady errant'.[1] Johnson rebuked Dryden for 'petulantly and

---

[1] 'Dedication of the *Æneis*', *Essays*, edited by W. P. Ker, second impression, 1926, ii. 165.

indecently' denying 'the heroism of Adam, because he was overcome', and asserted that there was 'no reason why the hero should not be unfortunate, except established practice, since success and virtue do not go necessarily together'. Dryden's other complaint, that the subject necessitated more 'machining' (supernatural) persons than human, was taken up by Johnson who complained that 'the want of human interest is always felt'.[1] But Johnson, like Dryden, made no complaint against Milton for making the Deity an actor in his epic, or against the manner in which the Deity is presented. Nor does he complain of Milton's exposition of the Divine Economy through the mouth of its author. He exempts the Father and Son from discussion as not being characters 'which admit of examination'; but it would be wrong to deduce from this that Johnson shared a later view that blamed Milton for making them actors in his epic, or that he shared later dissatisfaction with Milton's presentation of the Father in act and speech. Instead he praises Milton's moral purpose as 'the most useful and the most arduous', the construction of the 'fable', in which Milton has 'interwoven the whole system of theology with such propriety, that every part appears to be necessary', and the greatness of the subject and of the persons.

It was Blake the heretic and Shelley the philosophic agnostic who first saw a difference between Milton's avowed purpose and his actual accomplishment and applauded Milton for doing something other than what he declared that he intended to do and what Marvell and Johnson thought that he had done. Blake's statement that

[1] 'Milton', *Lives of the Poets*: 'The plan of *Paradise Lost* has this inconvenience, that it comprises neither human actions nor human manners. The man and woman who act and suffer, are in a state which no other man or woman can ever know. The reader finds no transaction in which he can be engaged; beholds no condition in which he can by any effort of imagination place himself; he has, therefore, little natural curiosity or sympathy.'

The reason Milton wrote in fetters when he wrote of Angels & God, and at liberty when of Devils & Hell, is because he was a true Poet and of the Devil's party without knowing it,

requires for full understanding consideration of Blake's whole philosophic system; but taken at its simplest it implies that only certain parts of Milton's poem are the work of a 'true poet', the product of a freely creative imagination, and that the rest are the work of the reason that divides and distinguishes, fettering the creative energies of the imagination and presenting the abstractions of intellect rather than the living truths of the poetical genius. Shelley went further, claiming that *Paradise Lost* 'contains within itself a philosophical refutation of that system of which, by a strange and natural antithesis, it has been a chief popular support'; he praised Milton for his 'bold neglect of a direct moral purpose' in having 'alleged no superiority of moral virtue to his god over his devil'. Milton, he declared, did not follow a didactic purpose but 'the laws of epic truth' by which 'a series of actions of the external universe and of intelligent and ethical beings is calculated to excite the sympathy of succeeding generations of mankind'.[1] That is, Milton designed his fable and created his persons so as to commit it and them to the free moral judgement of mankind. And Shelley was in no doubt as to what that judgement should be. In refusing to make his God morally superior to his Devil, Milton, said Shelley, 'violated the popular creed', but he added a significant parenthesis: 'if this shall be judged to be a violation.' What Shelley only hinted Professor Empson has said flatly. The merit of *Paradise Lost*, to him as to Shelley, is that it exposes with such clarity the hatefulness of Christianity as a theological system. He sees Milton as a great and generous soul struggling to moralize or

[1] 'A Defence of Poetry' in *Four Ages of Poetry*, edited by H. F. B. Brett-Smith, 1921, pp. 46–47.

render just tolerable an essentially immoral and intolerable creed:

> The reason why the poem is so good is that it makes God so bad.
> . . . Milton has stretched his historical imagination very far. The poem really does survey the Western half of civilization and express the conflict which arose from the introduction of Christianity into this great area, as a by-product of offering a solution to it which seems to him tolerably decent. The root of his power is that he could accept and express a downright horrible conception of God and yet keep somehow alive, underneath it, all the breadth and generosity, the welcome to every noble pleasure, which had been prominent in European history just before his time.[1]

Professor Empson's book is a response that was, I think, to be expected to trends in Milton scholarship and Milton criticism in the last twenty years. The nineteenth and the early twentieth centuries accepted on the whole Blake's distinction between Milton the poet and the Milton who wrote in fetters, and were content to enjoy the one and to mock slyly at the other. The dominant religious attitude among intellectuals was Liberal Christianity which stressed the beauty of the ethical teaching of the Gospels and concerned itself with problems such as their historicity, the philosophy of miracles, and the truth of the Christian hope of a future life, rather than with theology proper. Apart from the disappearance of belief in the Scriptural narrative of creation and the very existence of any such persons as our first parents, the Old Testament as a whole was regarded with considerable distaste, and a constant distinction was drawn between the God of the Old Testament and the God of the New. The Liberal or the 'Modern' Churchman joined hands here with the Anglo-Catholic whose theological concerns were very different from Milton's and who had a natural dislike for so inveterate a hater of bishops. T. S. Eliot, who could not be described as a Liberal Churchman, gave expression

---

[1] *Milton's God*, 1961, pp. 275 and 276–7.

to what I remember as a current view of the value of *Paradise Lost* as an exposition of the Christian Faith when I was young:

> I cannot feel that my appreciation of Milton leads anywhere outside of the mazes of sound. . . . So far as I perceive anything, it is a glimpse of a theology that I find in large part repellent, expressed through a mythology which would have been better left in the Book of Genesis, upon which Milton has not improved.[1]

My own tutor at Oxford, a devout Christian of the old-fashioned High Church kind, regarded Milton's theology with profound distaste and deflected her pupils from any discussion of it. In this intellectual atmosphere Christians and non-Christians alike could agree to dismiss Milton's system as a historic fossil embedded in the living beauty of his poem and admire him as an artist, sympathize with him as a champion of liberty, if the writer were in sympathy with the 'Good Old Cause', and ignore or deplore his theological concerns.[2]

A striking feature of the last thirty years has been the revival of belief in dogmatic Christianity and the revival of Biblical Theology. This has been very marked among men of letters and in the universities, and from there has permeated intellectual and cultural life. Theology has become a subject of dinner-table conversation, the plots of novels turn on theological points, the reviewers

[1] 'A Note on the Verse of John Milton', *Essays and Studies* (1935), 1936, p. 38. In the same essay, in which Eliot declared that as a man Milton 'is antipathetic', he dismissed his claims to intellectual respect as well as his 'likeableness': 'Either from the moralist's point of view, or from the theologian's point of view, or from the psychologist's point of view, or from that of the political philosopher . . . Milton is unsatisfactory' (p. 32).

[2] Mr. Cardan in Aldous Huxley's *Those Barren Leaves*, 1925, expresses the view of the twenties very well: 'The theological and, to Milton himself, the fundamental and essential part of *Paradise Lost* is now so ludicrous that we ignore it altogether. When somebody speaks of Milton, what do we call to mind? A great religious poet? No. Milton means for us a collection of isolated passages, full of bright light, colour and thunderous harmony, hanging like musical stars in the lap of nothing.'

in the Sunday papers and the weeklies have Original Sin
and Grace readily on their lips, and every first-year
student of English can at need bring the Fall or the Loss
of Eden into the discussion of the play, or novel, or lyric
which is the subject of the weekly essay and spot 're-
deemer figures'. Behind this popular interest there lies an
intellectual revolution. The myths of Genesis and the
legends of Jewish history embedded in Genesis and
Exodus have resumed their power over men's imaginations. Rejected as history they have returned as myths,
valued for their symbolic meaning as expressive of the
human predicament and the divine response to it. Biblical
scholarship has made it clear that the New Testament
cannot be understood without the Old. The attempt to
isolate the Gospel message from the context in which it
was first preached and to ignore or depreciate the religious
experience and traditions in which Christ and his first
followers were brought up is now seen to have been an
aberration which ignored the facts of history. The old
antithesis between the simplicities of the Gospel and the
theological subtleties of Paul has been abandoned. It is
now recognized that the evangelists were theologians too.
A parallel movement, which has drawn strength from
and given strength to the achievements of Biblical scholarship, and has had an even wider popular influence, is the
concentration of art-historians on iconography. We have
been familiarized, by being shown their presence in works
of present power, with conceptions that our grandfathers,
and even our fathers, thought wholly grotesque and outmoded. In addition, historical scholarship in its fight with
New Criticism has found common ground in the belief
that works of art should be regarded as wholes. In such
a climate of opinion, discussion of *Paradise Lost* has become discussion of the poem as a unity, and Milton's
avowed intention, the value of his thought, and his success
in his declared purpose have become centres of interest.

Powerful, learned, and persuasive writers have set *Paradise Lost* before us as a classic expression of Christian Humanism, its main thesis still relevant today. Although some lonely voices, notably Professor Haller's, are raised to give it a more limited significance as the 'Epic of Puritanism', the more common orthodox view has been that expressed by the late Professor C. S. Lewis when he wrote that 'as far as doctrine goes, the poem is overwhelmingly Christian. Except for a few isolated passages it is not even specifically Protestant or Puritan. It gives the great central tradition.'[1]

In opposition to these 'neo-Christians', as Professor Empson calls them (on analogy with the neo-Classics who are so much more orthodox than the Classics), and to the historical critics—they are often the same—there is another school of critics who also insist that we read the poem as a whole and not for its 'beauties', but who insist that we must not go outside the poem as it stands to make sense of what Milton has not made sense of, or to justify by pointing to sources and parallels what we do not find morally or artistically justifiable as we read. We ought, they hold, to read *Paradise Lost* as we read any work of fiction, by the light of our own experience of life and knowledge of the world, and to judge the acts and speeches of the characters by our own highest moral standards. The champion here was the late Professor Waldock,[2] to whom all critics of this school pay tribute, and who, it is constantly said, has never been answered. His platform was that we must judge Milton's poem by the effect it has on a reader of normal sensibility and moral feeling, taking Shelley's view that its God is no more beyond our judgement than Homer's Zeus or Virgil's Juno. The incidents and the characters must be judged as we judge the characters in any fiction, and the structure and design of the

---

[1] *A Preface to Paradise Lost*, 1942, p. 91.
[2] In *'Paradise Lost' and its Critics*, 1947.

whole by its internal coherence and conclusiveness. Waldock applied to *Paradise Lost* critical methods developed
from the criticism of novels and, as is well known, found
Milton an incompetent narrative artist, writing in the
infancy of the art of fictional narrative, who had chosen an
impossible subject to blow up to this size. The story in
Genesis, he declared, was like a stretch of film minutely
flawed. In enlarging it Milton made the flaw obvious and
disastrous to the whole. To Waldock the whole poem
collapses at the climax where Milton, far from carrying
the reader with him, provokes the contrary reaction to the
reaction his purpose demands. The moral sense of every
decent reader must approve Adam's decision to follow
Eve in eating the apple, for he is following here the highest
moral value we know—Love.

Professor John Peter has recently carried Waldock's
method yet further,[1] and by minute examination convicts
Milton again and again of inconsistencies and contra-
dictions (the 'fallacy of eating cake and having it too'), of
flagrant 'artistic opportunism' or 'effect-hunting', and of
failure to see the implications of episodes and incidents.
Why, he asks, are the assembled rebel angels seduced by
the patent sophistries of Satan and none of them convinced
by the much better arguments of Abdiel? 'Has Satan
somehow contrived to isolate Heaven's imbeciles, and is
a third of its population imbecile?' Milton had a fondness
for the situation of the one just man standing alone for
the truth, and 'in his excitement at Abdiel's solitary defiance' he has 'overlooked' the problem that arises 'con-
cerning all the other angels, whose loyalty, love, and zeal
appear to have been recklessly mislaid. Abdiel has to be
convincing, but the more convincing he is the more foolish,
or wicked, the others must appear.'[2] Professor Peter

---

[1] *A Critique of 'Paradise Lost'*, 1960.

[2] Professor Peter does not explain how a merely human intelligence, however
lofty, could invent arguments that would deceive superhuman minds.

discovers so many 'absurdities' of this kind as to provide by himself a refutation of his critical approach. Although we may all agree that Homer sometimes nods and that it is a critic's duty to note these lapses, there must surely be something wrong with the demands we are making on a work of art if the result of our examination is to show Homer permanently half-asleep.

Professor Empson is the latest recruit to the Waldock camp, and he has employed the method of free inquiry into 'what Milton actually does in *Paradise Lost*' with his own characteristic intellectual ingenuity. He treats the poem as if it were a rather subtle detective story whose point we can only discover by alertness in picking up small clues. He finds, for instance, that although God supposedly sent Raphael to warn Adam and Eve against eating the fruit, his narrative is in fact a subtle incitement to Eve to perform this dangerous act, and is designed to make her think that, in spite of the prohibition, God really wants her to do it. If we read the poem thus, with close attention, we shall be able to spot the real criminal, and, as in all the best detective stories, he will be the most obviously unlikely candidate—God.

As Donne observed,

They beare most blows which come to part the fray.

I have little hope that a middle position will win much favour from either side. But when I read Charles Williams, C. S. Lewis, and Douglas Bush on the one side and Waldock, Peters, and Empson on the other, I feel I am reading about a rather different poem from the poem that I have read and loved since childhood. Those who set *Paradise Lost* before us as a classic expression of Christian Humanism are inclined to use it as a pretext for sermons on the sins of today and to suggest that dissent from, or dissatisfaction with, Milton's presentation of the scheme of things, or rather with their interpretation of Milton's presentation, is the result of some moral obliquity in the reader, resenting the exposure of his own cherished weaknesses. I feel a certain disregard among these critics of Shelley's claim that *Paradise Lost* 'obeys the laws of epic truth', and that in place of a stupendous and liberating work of the imagination I am being presented with a massive cautionary tale. I hasten to add that many of the sermons that have been preached to me out of *Paradise Lost* are beautiful, sometimes subtle and searching, and I do not wish to question their salutariness. But, to give examples, C. S. Lewis's discussion of the varieties of evil disposition shown in the great 'consult' of Book II seems to range very far from what the text presents to our imagination. Is it right to compare the Belial who can exclaim

> for who would loose,
> Though full of pain, this intellectual being,
> These thoughts that wander through Eternity,

with a man who intends to 'grow numb, voluntarily to decline on to a lower plane of being . . . to avoid great literature and noble music and the society of uncorrupted men as an invalid avoids draughts?'[1] Must we tie Milton at every point to a direct exemplary purpose and not allow him to find and present to us gleams of nobility of mind and of heroic virtue among these generals debating what course they should adopt after a shattering defeat? If we do, we ignore Milton's own clear comment:

> neither do the Spirits damn'd
> Loose all thir vertue.[2]

Again, Professor Lewis's analysis of the successive sins that Eve falls into, ending with Murder, presents us with the abstractions and exaggerations of the moralist in place

---

[1] *A Preface to 'Paradise Lost'*, p. 103.
[2] *P.L.* II. 482–3.

of Milton's presentation of excitement, elation, momen-
tary desire for separateness and superiority, immediate
realization of the peril she has incurred, with the hateful
thought of Adam living on without her, happy with
'another Eve', and final resolution, in which she seems to
express the whole truth of her nature:

> *Adam* shall share with me in bliss or woe:
> So dear I love him, that with him all deaths
> I could endure, without him live no life.

Are these lines really to be read as Eve 'congratulating
herself' upon having planned Adam's death 'as a singular
proof of the tenderness and magnanimity of her love'?[1]
Such comments seem more concerned with the reader's
morals than with Milton's meaning.

The critics of the opposite school, who demand that
Paradise Lost should stand the test of the kind of close
reading that we give to a novel by Jane Austen or Henry
James, show an equal though dissimilar disregard for the
laws of epic truth, which are not the same as the laws of
prose fiction. They refuse to make the initial act of generous willingness to concede the assumptions of the poet,
and the assumptions that he could rightly take for granted
as governing the minds of his readers, without which it is
impossible to receive, with any approach to fullness, what
works of past ages have to give. This willingness to concede is particularly necessary with epic poetry, which can
only exist on a basis of shared assumptions. It expresses
the ideals and beliefs that animate a culture, is comprehensive, not idiosyncratic, and sets forth truths held to be
universally valid. The epic poet does not write to convince doubters or to propagate individual views, but to
'assert'. It is, of course, just those matters which an age
assumes to be beyond questioning that later ages question,
and epic poetry demands therefore a greater effort of

---

[1] *A Preface to 'Paradise Lost'*, p. 121.

imagination and a greater willingness to grant the writer's premises than does drama or lyric poetry. The poetic greatness of *Paradise Lost* is in large measure due to the fact that Milton was able to take so much for granted. He was not writing a work of Christian apologetics on the one hand or a symbolic novel on the other. He was writing an epic poem, retelling the best-known story in the world, and a story whose main meaning and import he did not have to establish.

The way into the universe of *Paradise Lost*, the world created for our delight and instruction by Milton's imagination and his art, remains the same for the twentieth as for the seventeenth-century reader. It is the way that he provides by his exordium. He shows his awareness of the unprecedented boldness of his enterprise; and, adapting the age-old convention of the epic poet's address to the Muse, he reveals the mood in which he conceived, meditated, and finally brought to completion, his poem.

Of Mans First Disobedience, and the Fruit
Of that Forbidden Tree, whose mortal tast
Brought Death into the World, and all our woe,
With loss of *Eden*, till one greater Man
Restore us, and regain the blissful Seat,
Sing Heav'nly Muse, that on the secret top
Of *Oreb*, or of *Sinai*, didst inspire
That Shepherd, who first taught the chosen Seed,
In the Beginning how the Heav'ns and Earth
Rose out of *Chaos*: or if *Sion* Hill
Delight thee more, and *Siloa's* Brook that flow'd
Fast by the Oracle of God; I thence
Invoke thy aid to my adventrous Song,
That with no middle flight intends to soar
Above th' *Aonian* Mount, while it pursues
Things unattempted yet in Prose or Rhime.
And chiefly Thou O Spirit, that dost prefer
Before all Temples th' upright heart and pure,
Instruct me, for Thou know'st; Thou from the first

> Wast present, and with mighty wings outspread
> Dove-like satst brooding on the vast Abyss
> And mad'st it pregnant: What in me is dark
> Illumine, what is low raise and support;
> That to the highth of this great Argument
> I may assert Eternal Providence,
> And justifie the wayes of God to men.

Milton is following convention in opening with a synopsis of his argument, the plot of his poem. He departs from convention and begins the expansive movement so characteristic of his genius in his address to the Muse, whom Homer and Virgil invoke only briefly. The invocation to the Muse at the opening of the poem is the epic poet's way of declaring the importance and the truth of his subject. He is not going to make things up. He is going to relate what the Muse has revealed. Epic poetry must always make this claim; it is not fiction, it is true and it is important. It has been revealed to the poet who now reveals it to us. He speaks to us with authority greater than his own. But the Muse that Milton invokes is not one of the Nine, although she bears the name, as we learn in the prologue to Book VII, of the classical Muse of astronomy, Urania. It is the 'Heav'nly Muse' that Milton invokes, the Muse of sacred song and of prophecy, who inspired the poets and prophets of Israel, the Muse of divine inspiration who was before the world began, sister of the Eternal Wisdom who played with her before the throne of the Eternal Father. Milton's Muse is the source of all human knowledge of divine things and of human power to utter them.

In the *De Doctrina Christiana* Milton declared that to know God as he is transcends the powers of human thought, much more of human perception, and added:

Our safest way is to form in our minds such a conception of God, as shall correspond with his own delineation and representation of

himself in the sacred writings. For granting that both in the literal
and figurative descriptions of God, he is exhibited not as he really is,
but in such a manner as may be within the scope of our comprehen-
sions, yet we ought to entertain such a conception of him, as he, in
condescending to accommodate himself to our capacities, has shewn
that he desires we should conceive (Book I, chapter ii).

Scripture in what it tells us of God is a sacred and inspired
fiction. The Heavenly Muse is the inspirer of the writers
of Scripture, communicating to them and through them
true knowledge of God in forms comprehensible to the
human intellect, helping them to 'imitate', as Sidney said,
'the inconceivable excellencies of God'.

Following ancient tradition, by which classical deities
were invoked under different names and at various sanctuaries, Milton invokes his Muse first as inspirer of
Moses who, in the forty days and nights when he was
alone on Mount Sinai, hidden in cloud, was thought to
have learned not only the law but also those secrets of
creation that he revealed in Genesis. Then he invokes her
as haunting the waters of Siloah that flow beneath Mount
Sion on which stood the Temple that contained the 'Oracle
of God', the Ark of the Covenant, the sign of God's perpetual presence with his people. The waters of Siloah, like
the Pierian springs, spring out from beneath a hill on
which, like Mount Olympus, the supreme deity has his
seat. In these waters Jesus told the blind man, whose eyes
he had anointed with clay and spittle, to wash his eyes.
They are thus a fit haunt for the Muse that reveals. Two
mountains of revelation are set before us: Sinai, where in
cloud and storm Moses received a special revelation, and
Sion, where God tabernacled with men, to be found by
those who sought him. Inspiration is given unsought to
those who are called to receive it. It is also to be sought
where God has promised that it shall be found.

How are we to regard Milton's invocation of the Muse?
Is she a metaphor for the Holy Spirit? Surely not; for he

turns from his invocation of the Muse to a prayer to the Spirit, which is in quite a different tone. She is also, surely, more than a mere personification of one of the gifts of the Spirit. Personifications are not addressed with such ardour and reverent warmth. One might say paradoxically that the address to the Muse is a convention with the pagan poets Homer and Virgil, but with the Christian Milton it is not. Has she then a metaphysical reality? Does Milton believe intellectually in the existence of a Heavenly Muse, as men have believed in angels, or as the Neoplatonists believed in 'emanations', mediatory spiritual beings between the divine and the human in the scale of being? I think we must reject this notion too. The Heavenly Muse has no status within the epic itself. She is inseparable from the poet, and is no part of the universe he presents to us. She has another kind of reality. In his invocation to her Milton has summed up all his feeling about the sacredness of his vocation, the reality of his calling, and the truth of his subject, all his awe at his own temerity and his sense that through him great things are to be said. In invoking her aid he expresses also his sense that although he goes forward alone 'in darkness, and with dangers compast round', he is not alone; he has great allies, others before him and others who will come after him 'smit with the love of sacred song'. Through his invocation of her he declares that inspiration is a reality, not a subjective fancy. She is the poetic embodiment of Milton's belief in his vocation, no more a convention than those 'Powers' that haunt the poetry of Wordsworth.[1]

[1] Cf.   Imagination—here the Power so called
Through sad incompetence of human speech,
That awful Power rose from the mind's abyss
Like an unfathered vapour that enwraps,
At once, some lonely traveller (*Prelude*, Book VI).

By a phrase that follows, 'in such strength of usurpation', Wordsworth makes clear that his 'Imagination' is more than a mere faculty of the individual mind.

From the Muse of Sinai and of Sion Milton turns to pray to the Spirit, and I suppose everyone who reads this prelude to the poem must be struck by the contrast between the tone and rhythms of the first sixteen lines— one great rolling sentence with suspended verbs, culminating in the tremendous aspiration to pursue

> Things unattempted yet in Prose or Rhime—

and the tone and rhythms of the prayer that follows, with its briefer clauses, simpler syntax, and solemn balance:

> What in me is dark
> Illumine, what is low raise and support;

and

> I may assert eternal Providence
> And justifie the wayes of God to men.

The invocation to the Muse is full of confidence and daring, and this same note recurs in the prologues to Books III and VII when the Heavenly Muse is again invoked.[1] The prayer to the Spirit is a genuine prayer, rooted as all prayer must be in humility.

In the twenty-six lines of his exordium Milton shows the range of the grand style he is to adopt by touching both its poles. In a series of articles in the *Sunday Times*, expanded into his book *Looking at Pictures* in 1960, Sir Kenneth Clark chose Raphael's cartoon of *The Miraculous Draught of Fishes* in the Victoria and Albert Museum to teach us how, if we are 'calm enough or strong enough to make the effort', we can 'participate in the strenuous life of the Grand Manner'. The world of Raphael's picture is, he says,

a world as far from actual experience as the language and images of Milton are far from every-day speech. Whatever the original episode

---

[1] It is absent from the prologue to Book IX, where Milton changes his 'Notes to Tragic' and comes to the heart of the human theme of his poem. Here he does not invoke the Muse, but humbly hopes that she may grant him 'answerable style'.

Raphael: The Miraculous Draught of Fishes
(*Victoria and Albert Museum: Crown Copyright*)

in St. Luke's Gospel was like, it was not like this, and Raphael never supposed that it was. But he was treating a great theme, and decorating the most splendid room in Christendom, and in consequence every figure and every incident must be made as noble as the story would allow. What did he mean by that word? Looking at the *Miraculous Draught*, I see that the figures are robust and handsome specimens of humanity. . . . They have no hesitations, nor secret thoughts, but stand up in the open and concentrate wholeheartedly on what they are doing. But this condition of being is achieved through style. Just as Miltonic diction could raise almost every episode to a certain level of nobility, so Raphael's power of finding a simple, comprehensible and well-shaped equivalent for everything he saw gives an elevated unity to the whole scene.

Sir Kenneth says that without this unity of style he would be disturbed by the fact that the two groups in the painting 'are conceived in different moods'. The group on the right, of Zebedee and his two sons, represents 'art for art's sake'. In the two sons bending over their nets, Raphael 'is consciously giving a proof of his mastery of *disegno*, that key word of the Renaissance which meant drawing, design and formal conviction all in one'. Zebedee is 'intended to recall an antique river god; and the whole splendid boatful is addressed to the connoisseur, whom it cannot fail to please as long as there survives any memory of the classic tradition'. The group in the left-hand boat, on the other hand, Christ, Peter, and Andrew,

is addressed to the believer. 'Depart from me; for I am a sinful man, O Lord.' By this profoundly human response to a piece of miraculous good fortune Raphael's imagination has been touched and quickened so that style no longer dominates truth.

But having made this distinction between a triumph of art and a triumph of truth, Sir Kenneth draws back to elucidate the unity of the whole composition which can include, by a 'rhythmic cadence' running through the whole, the artist's passion for beautiful forms and the artist's response to profound human emotion. He notes the 'marvellous acceleration' of this rhythm in the figures of the praying St. Peter, 'to whose passionate movement all these devices have been a preparation, and finally the comforting figure of Christ, whose hand both checks and accepts St. Peter's emotion'.[1]

I am delighted to be allowed to cite this analysis of a great picture. It is deeply relevant to *Paradise Lost* as I now see it, and the phrase that Sir Kenneth uses of the mature Raphael, 'his unrivalled powers of assimilation', is equally applicable to Milton. The contrast Sir Kenneth points to between the group that appeals to our sense of beauty and tradition and the group that 'speaks to the believer' is the same contrast as we are aware of in moving from Milton's confident invocation of the Muse of Divine Poetry to his prayer to the Spirit who prefers above all sanctuaries the 'upright heart and pure'. From Sinai and Sion, sources of those divinely inspired fictions by which the truth of things is shadowed to the imagination and intellect, we move to the believer's chamber where man in secret implores the help of the Spirit. From the thought of what is to be the material of great art, the 'great Argument' or plot of the poem, Milton's mind turns to what he dares hope will be the great religious truth that his poem will 'assert'.

It is usual to quote the last line of the exordium when discussing Milton's didactic aim and to say that he wrote *Paradise Lost* to 'justifie the wayes of God to men'. This is an impressive amplification, a variation for emphasis and to give rhythmic finality, of the clause in the line before where he prays that he may 'assert Eternal Providence'. 'Eternal Providence' is the motivating religious theme of the whole poem, and this word, which ends the penultimate line of the exordium, is repeated at the close of the whole poem as man and woman go out from Eden

[1] *Looking at Pictures*, 1960, pp. 63–67.

into the world we know and the history of humanity
begins:

> The World was all before them, where to choose
> Thir place of rest, and Providence thir guide:
> They hand in hand with wandring steps and slow,
> Through *Eden* took thir solitarie way.

This exquisite quiet close, a conclusion in which nothing
is concluded, takes its touching pathos from the word
'solitarie'. Without angelic guard or visible protection,
defended only by the consolation of mutual love, man and
woman are seen as small and lonely figures moving out into
the world of time. And yet they are not solitary if Milton
has succeeded in reaffirming to the satisfaction of the
heart and imagination the doctrine of God's constant care
for mankind. It is this doctrine that Milton prays his
retelling of the great story will display, and here that he
hopes, while delighting the connoisseur, to 'speak to the
believer'.

I do not believe that Milton embarked on his poem in
the belief that he could solve the intellectual problems
and difficulties that are inherent in belief in the doctrine
of Providence. But neither do I believe that he was unaware of these difficulties. The intellectual and moral
difficulties involved in the belief that the will of God is the
final activating cause of all that happens and all that exists
are only too obvious and can be exposed by any sharp-
witted schoolchild. To believe that God is omnipotent,
that his purposes cannot be frustrated, and yet that his
creatures are free to act as they choose and are to be held
responsible for their actions is to believe what is, however
the theologians argue it, on the face of it a logical contradiction. To take refuge in a 'God of the Philosophers'
who does not know the world and neither created it by an act
of will nor takes any interest in its history relieves the mind,
as R. G. Collingwood observed, of 'many embarrassments':

It relieves us of the necessity to think of God as beholding and tolerating, or still worse as deliberately causing, the evils of which the world is full, which is always a grave moral difficulty to the popular Christian theology; and it relieves us of the necessity to think of Him as seeing colours, hearing sounds, and so forth, which would imply His having eyes and ears, or alternatively as knowing a world so different from ours that we can no longer call it by the same name.

But, Collingwood added, 'although these are great gains, they are offset by what we cannot but feel to be greater losses':

The thought of God as watching over the life of the world, directing the course of its history, judging its actions, and bringing it ultimately back to unity with Himself, is a thought without which we can hardly care to think of God at all.[1]

The fallen angels, it will be remembered, 'reason'd high'

Of Providence, Foreknowledge, Will, and Fate,
Fixt Fate, free will, foreknowledge absolute,
And found no end, in wandring mazes lost.

Though these are fallen, they are still intellectual beings who 'reason high'. Milton, who had a noble confidence in reason's power, here clearly implies its limits, as he does again in *Paradise Regained* when speaking of the ancient philosophers whose 'conjectures' and 'fancies' were 'built on nothing firm':

Ignorant of themselves, of God much more,
And how the world began, and how man fell
Degraded by himself, on grace depending.
Much of the Soul they talk, but all awrie,
And in themselves seek vertue, and to themselves
All glory arrogate, to God give none,
Rather accuse him under usual names,
Fortune and Fate, as one regardless quite
Of mortal things.[2]

1 *The Idea of Nature*, 1945, reprinted Galaxy Books 1960, p. 88.
2 *Paradise Regained*, IV. 310–18.

It is in the revelation that God does 'regard' mortal things that Milton finds the difference between the wisdom of the ancients and the wisdom of the Bible.

If, as I have said, I am unable to believe that when Milton declared that his purpose was 'to assert Eternal Providence' he thought of himself as providing a solution to the difficulties inherent in the Biblical doctrine of God that would satisfy the unaided reason, I am also unable to believe that he was happily unaware of the dilemma that the rendering of this conception in epic form inevitably posed. Indeed, far from trying to disguise the problem, he again and again obtrudes it on the reader. Instead of seeing Milton as obtusely unconscious of what he was doing, blundering on in defiance of intellectual difficulties that are crystal clear to us, we should salute a moral and intellectual integrity that shirks none of the issues that faith in the God of Israel raises. Deeply as I disagree with much in Professor Empson's book, in this we are at one: in respecting and being moved by Milton's 'plain Heroic magnitude of mind', the generosity and intellectual candour that reigns in *Paradise Lost*. The dilemma he is in is obvious: on the one hand he risks showing God as 'mocked', on the other as 'mocking'. Either God is impotent in the face of disobedience and rebellion, or he is, as Professor Empson has said, a 'trickster' cheating his own troops in battle, giving Satan enough rope to hang himself, keeping fifth aces up his sleeve, and, most important of all, stage-managing the Fall of Man. It is, of course, the latter horn of this dilemma that Milton again and again impales himself on, as indeed he must. Even if his God the Father were more like the God whom men worship and less like a 'school-divine', less given to what Professor Empson calls 'blood-curdling jokes', this difficulty would remain. It is a waste of intellectual ingenuity to try to prove what Milton does not attempt to disguise: that the ultimate responsibility for the world as we know it, and therefore for all that happens in the poem, is God's. This Milton took for granted, and could assume that his readers would take for granted too, as he surely also took for granted that God was, by definition, good. He showed his courage and intellectual honesty by facing the implications of a belief in the God of Israel who 'visits and redeems his people', and in a God whose will was 'free to act or not' and who had created beings in his own image dowered with the same freedom.

I cannot believe that Milton dedicated himself to the writing of his epic in the hope that he might in the writing of it convince himself and his readers of the 'reasonableness of Christianity'. Instead I believe that he chose this subject as allowing him the greatest possible scope for imagination and invention on the basis of known and accepted truths. Instead of concentrating on the difficulties of the subject, criticism is better employed in seeing what Milton made of its vast opportunities. The particular emphasis that he gave to the story, the particular stress he laid, was partly that of his age; more importantly, it was that of his own individual mind and temperament. The stress of his age is something that we must allow; his own stress is what still speaks to us. In many ways Milton stands apart from concerns that we think of as characteristic of the seventeenth century. The great points at issue between the different confessions, turning on the doctrine of the Atonement, the relation of faith and works, church order, and the nature of the sacraments, are marginal to the true subject of *Paradise Lost*. And if we think of seventeenth-century religious writing we must be struck by how little some of the great seventeenth-century topics are reflected in Milton's poetry. The sense of sin, the need for salvation, the shudder at death, the fear of judgement, and the hope of resurrection—these are not themes that receive grand expression in *Paradise Lost*. Neither in his poetry nor in his prose do we ever hear in Milton's voice that thrilling note of personal anguish that gives the religious poems and the sermons of Donne the power to speak to those who may not share his faith but recognize the reality of his predicament. Milton shares with his age certain conceptions that are today quite unacceptable: an equation of sin with guilt, an outmoded psychology that makes him unable to conceive of temptation and sin in any but intellectual terms, and a narrowly legalistic theory of the Atonement. It is not in its presentation of these commonplaces of seventeenth-century theology and thought that the greatness of *Paradise Lost* lies, but in the fervour and the force with which Milton expressed certain personal convictions.

The doctrines to which Milton gives grand expression are of God's goodness and overflowing bounty in creation, of his mercy to fallen man, and of his will and power to bring good out of evil. It is in man's response to the divine bounty and to the divine mercy that the religious feeling of the poem is purest and strongest, as its ethical and moral force lies in the strength with which it affirms the freedom of the will, with the consequent dignity that this bestows on man as a responsible being, and the beauty with which it displays the joys and consolations of mutual love. Such dark questions as to why an ill will arose among the angels, natives of heaven, the poem is not concerned to answer. It was witty of Grierson to observe that 'if the third part of a school or college or nation broke into rebellion we should be driven, or strongly disposed, to suspect some mismanagement by the supreme power';[1] but this is a comment we could make on the story however it was treated if we will not grant the premise on which the whole story rests: that God is the Creator of angels as of men. He is not to be compared to a vice-chancellor whose credentials a professor doubts.[2] The story of the Fall of the Angels does

[1] H. J. C. Grierson, *Milton and Wordsworth*, 1937, p. 116.
[2] See Empson, *Milton's God*, p. 95.

nothing to explain the mystery of the origin of evil. It merely declares that evil is something more than human, that it is a cosmic force. Milton could rely here, as he could throughout his poem, on what Grierson elsewhere calls 'an unbounded reverence for the Bible', and invent and elaborate on a base that he could not imagine would ever be questioned. He knew that the whole story was in a sense a fiction, a divinely inspired fiction as he believed. The God of the Bible, and the God of his poem, was not the God who dwells in light inaccessible, who is 'higher than our highest thoughts and more inward than our inmost', but an image of him, capable of being grasped by minds living in space and time. Throughout his poem he reminds us of the existence, behind the drama he presents, of this God 'dark with excessive bright'. He can no more have thought the Father of his poem to be God as He is than Michelangelo can have thought his mighty Ancient creating Adam to be anything but a faint image of the Author of all being. To think of Milton as conceiving of God as the strategist and ironist of his poem is as naïve as to think of Michelangelo as believing that God possessed a pair of powerful legs. Both Milton and Michelangelo had to accept the limitations of their art, through which they expressed conceptions beyond the reach of narrative and pictorial images. I think we read *Paradise Lost* best if we read it in the spirit in which we look at great Renaissance paintings of Christian subjects. Much modern criticism of the poem seems to me as beside the point as asking, when we look at a superb painting of the Adoration of the Magi, how these magnificent figures have managed to traverse the snowy landscape in the background without getting snow on their boots, or complaining as we look at a painting of the Assumption of the Virgin that the artist still has not managed to convince us of the possibility of solid bodies being suspended in mid air without visible means of support.

II

THE UNIVERSE OF
PARADISE LOST

Every great work of art creates its own universe that obeys its own imaginative laws. As we read on, or look, or listen, we come to learn what may be expected and what may not, what we can demand and what we cannot or should not ask. It is in this sense that I wish to discuss the universe of *Paradise Lost*: what Milton's imagination has created, not his cosmology.

The universe of *Paradise Lost* is intensely dramatic. It is filled with energies and wills. As Milton himself tells us, he was a long time choosing the subject for his epic and late in beginning to write his 'Heroic Song'. We know that the subject that he took for his epic first pleased him as a subject for a tragedy, and that he made no less than four drafts for a tragedy on the Fall of Man many years before he took up the same subject for his epic. Apart from the testimony of his nephew that he had seen the opening of Satan's soliloquy on Mount Niphates as written for the beginning of a tragedy 'about 15 or 16 yeares before ever his Poem was thought of', there are many passages in *Paradise Lost* that correspond to episodes in Milton's most detailed synopsis of his projected tragedy and may well have been written for the tragedy that Milton abandoned and adapted for incorporation in his epic. But it is not the presence of these possible fossils from the projected tragedy that makes *Paradise Lost* so dramatic, for what strikes us at once about the drafts that Milton made for a tragedy on the Fall of Man is how undramatic they are,

and how undramatic this subject would necessarily have
been if cast into strict dramatic form. For, although God
the Father may be an actor in an epic, he can hardly be
an actor on a stage; and the two chief characters have to
be kept from appearing until after they have fallen. While
a poet may suggest the glories of 'naked Majestie' and a
painter may present them in their ideal beauty, the dramatist has no such licence. Further, the classic limitation to
a single place, Paradise, reduces the cosmic struggle to
matter for choruses and a discourse of enmity between the
angelic guards and Lucifer. It is difficult to see how this
could be made more majestic and impressive on a stage
than any clash between human sentries and a discovered
spy. That Milton so obstinately persisted, some time early
in the 1640s, in attempting to shape a tragedy on this
unpromising subject shows how deeply the subject itself
engaged his imagination: that he had found the theme
on which he wanted to write.

The great defect of any subject drawn from British or
Saxon history to a man of European outlook like Milton
was its incurable provinciality. Who in the seventeenth
century outside these islands cared about Alfred or, even
more, about obscure British kings? Though Milton had
decided to write in English, in his own tongue for his
own people, he was a man of European culture. He must
have felt that the theme of the wars of Alfred against the
Danes was too narrow a subject for the world poem that
he aspired to write and that the story of Arthur was too
fabulous to be a vehicle of epic truth and seriousness. We
do not know at what precise moment the change came,
and Milton realized that the subject he had thought of for
his tragedy was the fit subject for his epic, that he had
found the hero he was looking for in the first man, the
prototype of humanity, that he would write the epic of
Everyman. But the fact that he had considered this subject so persistently as a tragic subject deeply affected his

handling of it in narrative form. Paradoxically, the great advantage of handling it in epic form was that it made possible a far more dramatic treatment of every element in the story than would have been possible within the limits of a drama.

Johnson, in speaking of the art of epic poetry, the invention of which he ascribes to Homer's 'vigour and amplitude of mind', includes as one of its main features 'the interposition of dialogue'. Dramatic immediacy is a quality of all epic, as distinct from romantic narrative. Epic poetry tends always to dramatic heightening, to presenting scenes in which the characters express their convictions, fears, hopes, and feelings in conflict with each other and in impassioned speech. But *Paradise Lost* is remarkable for the quite exceptional amount of debate, discussion, persuasion, and lament that it contains. A very large proportion of the poem is in direct speech. Such scenes as the opening conversation between Satan and Beelzebub, the debate in Hell, the defiance of Abdiel, the temptation of Eve, the quarrel between Adam and Eve, come to mind at once. But in addition to these scenes of dramatic conflict, presenting the clash of wills, Milton also makes an unprecedented use of soliloquy, the most striking feature of the Elizabethan drama. Satan has no less than five long soliloquies, almost as many as Hamlet, and Adam is allowed a hundred and twenty lines of solitary lament.

When he tried to cast his subject into dramatic form Milton was faced with the difficulty that his two main characters could not appear until after the crisis of the action. The character he had to begin with was Lucifer 'bewailing his overthrow and seeking revenge', and, according to his nephew, he began to write Lucifer's part. The intensely dramatic handling of the figure of Satan is a main cause of the extraordinary hold he has on the imagination. The direct presentation of his agony and loss, of his inveterate hatred against God and his malice towards man, belongs to the earliest beginnings of *Paradise Lost* in Milton's creative imagination. Satan has the objectivity of a dramatic figure, and resists all attempts to reduce him to a mere personification of evil. His peers are on the tragic stage.[1] Milton's debt to Spenser as a teacher is writ large in his works, and has been much discussed. His relation to the dramatists, and particularly to Shakespeare, has been less often considered.

The same intensely dramatic imagination is the source of some of the things that most offend in Milton's presentation of God the Father. In spite of Johnson, his 'character' in the poem demands discussion. He is conceived almost wholly in terms of Power and Will, omnipotent power and unlimited will, and he displays the scorn and derision that omnipotence isolated from other qualities must feel for lesser power that vainly threatens it. We may also add that he displays the variability of temper that is a mark of uncontrolled will. He is also much given to dramatic acts: the sudden exaltation of the Son, and the well-staged scene in Heaven when he asks for a volunteer to save mankind. Milton's imagination projects the eternal counsels of Heaven into dramatic moments in a time sequence, setting the drama of the Son's offer to save the world against the drama of Satan's offer to risk all to destroy it.

The whole structure and design of the poem also has the concentration of drama upon a single climax. Having first cast this subject into dramatic form, Milton was faced with the problem of converting a subject to which he had given the concentration of classical drama into a subject capable of filling the large, discursive form of classical epic. The direct action of *Paradise Lost* remains very slight for all its momentousness. It is essentially a dramatic

[1] These points are expanded in an article written in 1948 on 'Milton's Satan and the Theme of Damnation in Elizabethan Tragedy', printed in Appendix A.

action expanded. The only manner in which Milton could expand was by developing the character and role of Satan. He could not expatiate at any length on the life of Adam and Eve before the Fall. Like happy nations they have no history. Either he could expand by beginning with the Fall of the Angels and the Creation of the World, or he could keep to the dramatic scheme, beginning his story after the Creation, and tell of the Fall of the Angels and the Creation of the World in relations. To begin at the beginning with the exaltation of the Son would have been contrary to all epic precedent. The epic poet must begin *in medias res*. But Milton could have begun earlier in the story than he did without disobeying this law. He chose not to do so, preferring to devote part of his fifth, the whole of his sixth and seventh, and part of his eighth book to relation of what had passed before his action began and adding in addition, at the close, the epic poet's vision of future things, occupying half the eleventh and most of the twelfth book. Well over a third of *Paradise Lost* is thus related, not direct, action. Further, the entrance of the hero, that key figure of all epic poetry, is delayed until a quarter of the poem has passed. It is true that in the *Odyssey*, one of the most perfectly plotted of all narratives, the hero does not appear in person until the fifth book; but this is an exception to the epic poet's usual desire to bring his hero before the reader as soon as possible. To arouse expectation and to make long preparation for the chief character's appearance is a dramatic device.

The scheme of the poem as finally written has preserved the tragic poet's concentration on the single event, the crisis of the action. Everything points to the Fall, leads to it and from it. By so shaping his material Milton was able to set in the centre of his epic his cosmic theme of the revolt of the angels and the creation of the world, displaying the contrary energies of destruction and creation. But by making these tremendous events the subject of a relation he makes clear that it is the human theme that is the true theme of his poem, that 'Man's First Disobedience' is the moment to which everything tends. The Fall is plotted in Hell, it is foreseen and its remedy is found in Heaven, the central books with their long relations are the preparation of man for the supreme test of his will to love and obey his Maker. The whole drama hinges on two simple acts:

> So saying, her rash hand in evil hour
> Forth reaching to the Fruit, she pluck'd, she eat:

and

> She gave him of that fair enticing Fruit
> With liberal hand: he scrupl'd not to eat
> Against his better knowledge, not deceav'd,
> But fondly overcome with Femal charm.
> Earth trembl'd from her entrails, as again
> In pangs, and Nature gave a second groan,
> Skie lowr'd, and muttering Thunder, som sad drops
> Wept at compleating of the mortal Sin
> Original.[1]

These slight symbolic actions—a hand reaching out and plucking, a hand taking from another hand, a hand lifting fruit to the mouth, a second hand lifting fruit to the mouth —are the climax of the whole action and Milton does not adorn his climax. The storm that breaks is not a terrible storm: sky lowers, thunder mutters, a few sad drops fall. That is all. Long before the cinema was invented Milton anticipated one of its most thrilling methods: the panorama, an aerial view of a country or a city, the settling on a village or a street, then on a house, and then on a room in the house, and finally the focusing on some tiny significant act, the tearing of a letter, the lifting of a glass. Dramatic intensity can take two forms, a heightening of actions and of speech so that the imagination is taken by storm, or, if we have been sufficiently prepared, the naked

[1] *P.L.* IX. 780-1, 996-1004.

presentation of a slight but significant act. When at last we come to it, with the weight of the poem behind it, the undramatic presentation of this simple act of disobedience is profoundly dramatic.

But although the scheme of *Paradise Lost* has a dramatic concentration unprecedented in epic, it has also a wider scope in time and space than any other epic poem. It ranges from the height of Heaven to the depth of Hell, and from the beginning of things to their final end, taking as by right, within its dramatic scheme, licence to include, as its universal theme allows, *quicquid agunt homines*. It has at once a strict design and an immense discursiveness: at once focuses upon a single historic event and includes an encyclopedia of world history. And similarly, if one says that the first impression is of an extremely dramatic imagination at work, creating a universe full of independent energies and wills in which all is vital and vigorous, dowering its creations with an independent life so that they have an existence beyond their strict function in the plot, imagining even the landscape of Paradise as not a static picture of arranged beauties but a living vital organism, its rivers seeming to act of their own volition, its sun 'smiting' the fields, its trees weeping their odorous gums and balms, its beasts frisking in their play—one has then to say that the universe of *Paradise Lost* is wholly un-dramatic, because the dramatist himself defies the first rule of dramatic presentation by being himself present throughout, an actor in his own play. He is not merely present in the beautiful prologues in which, going beyond all epic precedent, Milton takes the reader into the sanctuary of his own hopes and fears and sorrows, but he is present, as producer or presenter of his own drama, on the stage throughout. His voice is heard in constant comment, which breaks out as if irresistibly:

> O shame to men! Devil with Devil damn'd
> Firm concord holds, men onely disagree

> Of Creatures rational, though under hope
> Of heavenly Grace; and God proclaiming peace,
> Yet live in hatred enmitie, and strife
> Among themselves, and levie cruel warres . . .[1]

or

> So little knows
> Any but God alone, to value right
> The good before him, but perverts best things
> To worst abuse, or to thir meanest use.[2]

It is heard also in such splendid passages as the great digression on married love, ending with the tender apostrophe

> Sleep on,
> Blest pair; and O yet happiest if ye seek
> No happier state, and know to know no more;[3]

in interpretation of what is said and done, attempting to manipulate our feelings and responses:

> Thus *Belial* with words cloath'd in reasons garb
> Counsel'd ignoble ease, and peaceful sloath,
> Not peace:[4]

and in a continual use of eulogistic and dyslogistic epithets. It is this highly unclassical involvement of Milton in his epic that disgusts such critics as Professor Yvor Winters, who complains: 'I find that I grow extremely tired of the meaningless inflation, the tedious falsification of the materials by way of excessive emotion.'[5] It has made others assert that Milton is the true hero of his own epic, conducting a war *à l'outrance* on Satan, the creature of his

---

[1] *P.L.* II. 496–501.   [2] *P.L.* IV. 201–4.
[3] *P.L.* IV. 773–5.   [4] *P.L.* II. 226–8.
[5] *Hudson Review*, Autumn 1956, quoted by Empson, *Milton's God*, p. 91. For a fuller treatment of Milton's involvement in his epic, see Louis L. Martz, *The Paradise Within*, New Haven, 1964, pp. 105–10. Professor Martz, justly to my mind, finds in this 'human, flexible, responsive voice . . . interpreting the discoveries of his "unpremeditated verse"' one of the great beauties of the poem.

own imagination. *Paradise Lost* infuses into its great im-
personal theme the most intense personal feeling, and the
poet deliberately aims at evoking an emotional response
in us. Milton is attempting to have the best of both worlds,
or, in Professor Peter's words, to 'have his cake and eat
it', all through the poem. He is attempting to combine
what might be thought contraries, to achieve two effects
usually thought incompatible: to secure the concentration
of drama while enjoying the discursiveness of epic and to
make us respond to the objectivity of an accepted historic
fable while engaging us personally in a story that expresses
the poet's personal feelings and personal views.

The same ambiguity appears in the treatment of time
and space. The direct action of the poem is, as I have said,
very brief, and Milton is precise here with the precision
of epic as opposed to the vagueness of romance. The time
of the story is, on the other hand, immeasurable, extending
backwards into the eternity before time was created and
forward into the eternity when time shall be no more. But
even here Milton does not hesitate, in the interests of his
drama, to impose a time scheme of some precision, beginning with the Day in Heaven on which the Father exalted
the Son. On the Night of that Day the rebellion of Satan
took place, and the next Day the war began. It raged for
three Days and on the third the Son issued forth and
overthrew the rebels. For nine Days they fell through
Chaos to the place prepared for them and for a further
nine Days they lay 'vanquisht, rowling in the fiery Gulfe'.
During this period the world was created in six Days,
followed by a Sabbath of rest and rejoicing, Adam explored
Paradise, named the beasts, discovered his loneliness, and
was given a companion, Eve.

On the nineteenth Day after his expulsion from Heaven
Satan lifts his head and speaks to Beelzebub, and the
direct action of the poem begins. All that is left vague
here is the time taken by the march of the fallen angels,

the building of Pandaemonium, and Satan's flight through Chaos to the world. But as soon as Satan arrives in the universe, dominated by its great luminary the Sun, a time scheme comes into operation, culminating in the one tremendous night that follows on the day of the Fall. On this night doom falls on Satan and his followers, metamorphosed into serpents, Sin and Death arrive on the earth, the angels push the poles of the earth athwart, bringing into being the world we know of mutability and decay, change of season, and variety of weather, and Adam and Eve are reconciled and implore mercy. The following day Michael descends to prepare Adam for the world of history, the angelic squadrons descend, and Adam and Eve are expelled from Paradise.

This time scheme is brief and firmly stated. Yet though the time-table can be worked out from the poem, the effect on our imaginations is very different. We have the impression of long time. Milton and his readers were well aware that the Days of Creation were not our days and that the Days and Nights of Heaven, such a 'Day' as that on which the Son was exalted, were days outside the sun's reckoning. But the constant use of the word 'Day' and of phrases such as 'Soon as midnight brought on the duskie houre', or

> Now Night her course began, and over Heav'n
> Inducing darkness, grateful truce impos'd,

or

> Two dayes are therefore past, the third is thine,

give the effect of a tight time scheme, which is then contradicted by the enormous events and the vast distances traversed. Similarly, when Adam speaks to Raphael of his feeling for Eve, or when Eve says to Adam 'With thee conversing I forget all time', they do not speak like persons who have only known each other for a few days. Milton equivocates here, again making the best of both worlds; he employs an apparently precise time scheme, yet makes his poem seem to include aeons and the sense of a long Paradisal time for his sinless pair. He imposes succession of time of Heaven, yet declares to us

> Immediate are the Acts of God, more swift
> Then time or motion;

then adding at once

> but to human ears
> Cannot without process of speech be told,
> So told as earthly notion can receave.[1]

Words move in time and Milton's poem must move in time, yet he continually suggests that the time of the poem is an illusion. Here again there are analogies in Elizabethan drama, in the double time of *Othello* and the change from winter to summer while Lear roves in his madness and Edgar guides blind Gloucester to their meeting.

The treatment of space, the geography of *Paradise Lost*, is equally equivocal. Again, in accordance with epic precedent, Milton is precise. At the beginning he commits himself to an exact measurement. He declares that the distance from Hell to Heaven is three times the distance from earth ('the Center') to the furthest pole of the created universe; Satan and his crew have

> their portion set
> As far remov'd from God and light of Heav'n
> As from the Center thrice to th' utmost Pole.[2]

This, as it occurs at the beginning of the poem, gives at once the sense of vast distance, as the parallel measurement of time

> Nine times the Space that measures Day and Night
> To mortal men, he with his horrid crew
> Lay vanquisht,[3]

---

[1] *P.L.* VII. 176–9.   [2] *P.L.* I. 72–74.   [3] *P.L.* I. 50–52.

gives us the sense of an intolerable prolongation of pain and stupor. Milton, as he plays us into his poem, is using our human measurement to convey vastness sensuously. If one looks up on a starry night, as we are invited to do, the distance seems infinite; to conceive of it tripled defeats our powers. It is, of course, a fallacy to think that the universe as conceived by the older astronomy was small and cosy, as it inevitably appears in plans and sketches, or that the earth bulked large in the old cosmic scheme. Modern astronomical measurements are on so different a scale that they mean nothing to the sensuous imagination; but the Ptolemaic system conceived of the earth as tiny, a mere speck, a dot compared with the vast encircling spheres. Thus Adam, speaking of the whole created universe, called as always 'the World' in *Paradise Lost*, refers to the earth itself as

> a spot, a graine,
> An Atom, with the Firmament compar'd
> And all her numberd Starrs, that seem to rowle
> Spaces incomprehensible,

and wonders that these glorious bodies should move

> meerly to officiate light
> Round this opacous Earth, this punctual spot.[1]

The difference between the old geocentric universe and the new heliocentric universe was not that one was small and the other large. It was that the first, though immense, was limited and therefore picturable and imaginable. It was bounded by the great outer shell of the Primum Mobile. Although Copernicus did not himself see the implications of his theory, the infinity of the universe had been argued by Milton's day, notably by Bruno. This new sense of an infinite universe is imaginatively present in *Paradise Lost*. Though Milton accepts for his basis the old concept of a finite universe, his original conception of

---

[1] *P.L.* VIII. 17–20, 22–23.

Chaos and the Great Deep out of which the universe was formed and in which it floats gives us the other concept of boundlessness, of vast measureless space where no sense of direction guides. The continual swing between the precise and the vague, the measurable and the immeasurable is a prime element in Milton's power over our imaginations. He continually satisfies and then defeats our powers of visualization.

The first measurement—that the distance of Hell from Heaven is three times as far as the distance to the poles of the stellar universe, far beyond the fixed stars of the galaxy —is meant to convey, as it does, a sense of immense distance. But anyone unwise enough to try to use it to construct a scale map of the universe of *Paradise Lost* would soon discover his error. In Book III it is true that again Milton conveys to us a sense of the vastness of the created universe when he describes Satan standing at the foot of the stair that leads from the outer shell of the universe to Heaven, gazing down through the spheres, making his way down through the constellations to the Sun and being then directed by Uriel to the Globe that is earth. But at the close of the previous book Milton had shrunk this whole stellar universe to the mere size of a star seen by the moon, when Satan battling his way up through Chaos sees 'farr off th'Empyreal Heav'n'

> And fast by hanging in a golden Chain
> This pendant world, in bigness as a Starr
> Of smallest Magnitude close by the Moon.[1]

Hell is plainly far further from Heaven than any measurement this tiny orb could provide. And yet again the distance shrinks to nothing more unimaginable than a wider Hellespont when we find Sin and Death building a causeway over this Chaos through which Satan had struggled.

Dante's Hell was in the centre of the earth, and it is a

---

[1] *P.L.* II. 1051-3.

commonplace of criticism since Macaulay to compare the vastness and indefiniteness of Milton's Hell with the precise geography of Dante's with its spatial bounds and mapped circles. Milton has moved Hell out into the infinite chaos, the Great Deep. He gives a logical reason for doing so in the prose argument to Book I: that Earth and the Heavens were not made until after the rebel angels had fallen to the place prepared for them. But the true reason is surely imaginative. Before Hell and the World existed there was infinite space, divided into Heaven, the Empyrean, and Chaos, the Great Deep. Out of this Chaos Hell is created as the abode of devils and the World as the home of man. This is Milton's most significant departure from orthodoxy in *Paradise Lost*, his rejection of the doctrine of creation *ex nihilo*. Milton's World was created from pre-existent infinite matter upon which God's goodness or creative power had not been exerted:

> Boundless the Deep, because I am who fill
> Infinitude, nor vacuous the space.
> Though I uncircumscrib'd my self retire,
> And put not forth my goodness.[1]

Milton's materialism runs very deep. It permeates his whole poem, making him willing to suggest that Heaven is more like earth than perhaps we think and to assert the corporeality of angels. Here it gives him the concept of an infinite cosmos, to contrast with his finite universe bounded by its outer shell. This ancient scheme Milton accepts for the geography of his epic. He could hardly do otherwise. It was hallowed by poets and belonged to the imagination of centuries of European thought and art. It consorted also, as Raphael, an excellent tutor in the subject, points out, with the evidence of our senses.[2] As far as

---

[1] *P.L.* VII. 168–71.
[2] Cf. *P.L.* VIII. 117–18:

> Not that I so affirm, though so it seem
> To thee who hast thy dwelling here on Earth.

we are concerned the earth is the centre of the universe, the point from which we observe; the sun for us rises and sets. We see it move across the heavens; we do not feel the earth turn. We have not abandoned in common speech the old terminology because we all now know that the sun does not rise and set and that the earth turns on its axis. The hero of Milton's poem is man. The universe of his poem must be geocentric as the poem is homocentric. But since the epic poet is the poet of truth and the revealer of true things, including knowledge of nature and the causes of things, Milton cannot ignore the great scientific movement of his day, and, in addition to setting his sphere-encircled earth within a limitless Deep, he puts into the mouth of Raphael a clear and convincing exposition of the heliocentric system.

This is the most stupendous example of the Miltonic volte-face in the poem. For the angel blandly tells us that the whole solid base of the poem, the map that we have by Book VIII become accustomed to and have taken for granted, may well be quite wrong. As Raphael speaks, the spheres, through which Satan and the angels (including Raphael himself) have made their way, dissolve as in a transformation scene. Milton calls the old system in question at the centre of his poem. Having done so he dismisses the question as unimportant, and for the rest of the poem assumes the physical basis he had queried. Just as his time is at once brief and precise, but also long and vague, his space is measurable and immeasurable, his universe is planned, but perhaps not so. This combination of the exact and the imprecise, the fixed and the fluid, seen in his handling of time and space, is of the essence of the Miltonic manner in the conduct of the narrative. Logical consistency is the last thing we should ask for when we enter the universe of *Paradise Lost*.

A lack of precision in his visual imagery was one of the main complaints that T. S. Eliot and others made against Milton. It is quite right to point to this and to contrast Milton, as Macaulay did before Eliot, with Dante. Macaulay, however, was content to make the comparison and did not feel compelled to chide Milton for not writing like Dante. It is one of the oddities of taste that the attack on Milton's dramatic impressionism went on side by side with the recovery of appreciation of the great masters of the baroque style in architecture, sculpture, and painting. Milton's grand manner was denigrated. He was accused of meaningless inflation, excessive emotionalism, and lack of clear detail; his vast glooms and bursts of brilliant light were ascribed by the more kindly to his weak eyesight rather than to the quality of his imagination; and the energy with which he assaults our feelings was deplored. At the same time, Bernini was being recognized as an artist of originality and integrity, and Caravaggio and his followers in the seventeenth century were discovered to be highly congenial to our taste. The drama, the expressiveness, the concentration on episodes, single moments of intense feeling, the attempt to do more than one thing at once: to make sculpture move and architecture dance, to combine weight and lightness, mass and fluidity, to express the inexpressible, to play tricks with light and darkness—all this we have come to find imaginatively satisfying in the baroque style, the child of the classical, but venturing far beyond its limits. Milton is an adventurer of this kind. As Johnson truly said: 'Of all the borrowers from Homer he is the least indebted.'

In his lecture on Milton as delivered to the British Academy in 1947, when he endeavoured to modify his earlier strictures, T. S. Eliot indulged in some detailed critical comment which he omitted when he reprinted this lecture in *On Poetry and Poets* in 1957.[1] He read the first

---

[1] The omission of nearly four pages from this lecture as originally printed is not consistent with the statement in the preface to *On Poetry and Poets* that 'each item is substantially the same as on the date of its delivery or first publication'.

description of Satan from Book I to praise what he described first as 'the happy introduction of so much extraneous matter' and then as 'inspired *frivolity*'—'an enjoyment
by the author in the exercise of his own virtuosity'. Earlier
in the lecture he had referred to the same passage in a
general comment on Milton's world:

> I do not think that we should attempt to *see* very clearly any
> scene that Milton depicts: it should be accepted as a shifting phantas-
> magory. To complain because we first find the arch-fiend 'chained
> on the burning lake', and in a minute or two see him making his
> way to the shore, is to expect a kind of consistency which the world
> to which Milton has introduced us does not require.

Eliot might perhaps have noted that Milton is careful to
tell us that Satan was set at liberty by 'all-ruling Heaven'
and that he sardonically reminds us again of this when Satan
and Beelzebub 'glorying to have scap't the *Stygian* flood'
attribute this to themselves as gods and to 'their own
recover'd strength' and not to 'the sufferance of supernal
Power'. Otherwise, his comment seems to me very just.
Milton does not trouble with ways and means: the chains
do not melt, or fall miraculously off, nor does some angel
descend into Hell armed with a pair of Heaven-forg'd
secateurs to cut them. First we have the picture of Satan
chained. Then Satan is free. The 'adamantine chains and
penal fire', the sloping flames, the 'singèd bottom all
involv'd with stench and smoak'—these things appear
and disappear according to whether Milton needs them or
not. The fallen angels move freely, and for most of the
time they give no appearance of being in pain. They are
not fixed for ever in terrible postures, as are the damned
in the *Inferno*. We are left to imagine how their angelic
beauty has been impaired; but there is no reason to suppose that Milton intends more than that the marks of
passion and evil will are scored on once calm, angelic
countenances. As Milton is so constantly compared with

Dante to Dante's advantage, it is worth saying here that
it is surely to Milton's credit that he showed so little
inventiveness in imagining tortures or degrading the
enemies of God and Man by showing them grotesquely
deformed and contorted. He preferred to show the courage
of his fallen angels in rising superior to fierce pain, without
expatiating on the pain.[1]

But although I agree with Eliot's description of Milton's world as a 'shifting phantasmagory', I cannot agree
when he goes on to say that Milton is not appealing to our
visual sense but to our ears, that 'the emphasis is on the
sound, not the vision, upon the word, not the idea'. Milton
continually appeals to our feelings, our moral and imaginative responses, and to the associations stored up in
our memories from our experience and our reading.[2] In
this first description of Satan he is concerned to arouse in
us sensations of awe and horror, of dismay and curiosity.
He calls on us to do the work as we read: to respond with
our imaginations. He is manipulating our feelings in
accordance with his own dictum: that poetry is something

[1] It is also surely to Milton's credit that he refrained from what might have
proved a temptation to a less lofty mind, suggesting what human beings would
in future provide citizens for the enormous empty regions of his hell.

[2] I am summarizing here what was finely said by Macaulay: 'The most
striking characteristic of the poetry of Milton is the extreme remoteness of the
associations by means of which it acts upon the reader. Its effect is produced, not
so much by what it expresses, as by what it suggests; not so much by the ideas
which it directly conveys, as by other ideas which are connected with them. He
electrifies the mind through conductors. The most unimaginative man must
understand the *Iliad*. Homer gives him no choice, and requires from him no
exertion, but takes the whole upon himself, and sets the images in so clear a light,
that it is impossible to be blind to them. The works of Milton cannot be com-
prehended or enjoyed unless the mind of the reader co-operate with that of the
writer. He does not paint a finished picture or play for a mere passive listener. He
sketches and leaves others to fill up the outline. He strikes the keynote, and expects
his hearer to make out the melody.' Macaulay also challenges, rightly I think,
the notion that Milton's muster rolls of names are included mainly for their
sound. The names, he says, 'are not always more appropriate or more melodious
than other names. Every one of them is the first link in a long chain of associated
ideas.' See *Critical and Historical Essays*, Everyman edition, i. 157–8.

less 'subtile and fine' than logic and rhetoric, 'more simple, sensuous and passionate';[1] that is, poetry appeals to the common experience of men, to their sensations and feelings, and to their passions. The essential power of the Miltonic style, as developed in *Paradise Lost*, lies in the manner in which the rhythm carries us from one weighty, emotive, or evocative word to the next. The highly individual syntax, the inversions, suspensions of the verbs, appositions, parentheses, and infolded clauses, the repetitions, variations, and turns on words, the 'sense variously drawn out from one Verse into another'—all these devices have the effect of insinuating into our minds a flux of feelings that cohere in a total impression. We can analyse logically, to our profit and pleasure, afterwards; but if we listen to a reader, or read aloud ourselves, the logical connectives and syntactical structure are not what the mind primarily responds to. They are like the strong foundations of a building, rather than, as in most poetry, like the building's visible structure.[2]

The first description of Satan does not demand from us that we attempt to envisage a static figure, something that we might draw, but that we feel certain emotions about Satan. Within the wide limits that the poet's control of the whole long winding sentence imposes, we are invited to respond with what associations words set up for us. We arrive at a concept rather than an image; though this concept has been created by many images that have passed through our minds as we read.

> Thus Satan talking to his neerest Mate
> With Head up-lift above the wave, and Eyes

[1] *Tractate on Education.*

[2] 'The connexion of the sentences and the position of the words are exquisitely artificial; but the position is rather according to the logic of passion or universal logic, than to the logic of grammar. Milton attempted to make the English language obey the logic of passion as perfectly as the Greek and Latin. Hence the occasional harshness in the construction' (Coleridge, *Miscellaneous Criticism*, edited by Raysor, 1936, pp. 163–4).

> That sparkling blaz'd, his other Parts besides
> Prone on the Flood, extended long and large
> Lay floating many a rood, in bulk as huge
> As whom the Fables name of monstrous size,
> *Titanian*, or *Earth-born*, that warr'd on *Jove*,
> *Briarios* or *Typhon*, whom the Den
> By ancient *Tarsus* held, or that Sea-beast
> *Leviathan*, which God of all his works
> Created hugest that swim th' Ocean stream:
> Him haply slumbring on the *Norway* foam
> The Pilot of some small night-founder'd Skiff,
> Deeming some Island, oft, as Sea-men tell,
> With fixed Anchor in his skaly rind
> Moors by his side under the Lee, while Night
> Invests the Sea, and wished Morn delayes:
> So stretcht out huge in length the Arch-fiend lay
> Chain'd on the burning Lake.[1]

The first adjectives are colourless, given weight by their
position and alliteration. Satan's body lies 'long and large',
extended on the Flood. But at once more than mere size
is in question. His bulk is 'huge', and the 'huge' is in itself terrifying and alarming. The 'huge' differs from the
'large', the 'big', or the 'great': it carries an immediate
suggestion of enormity and of threat, and this suggestion
Milton at once expands for us. Satan is

> in bulk as huge
> As whom the Fables name of monstrous size.

Then to the notion of hugeness—enormous terrifying
bulk—and monstrosity he adds another idea: Satan is as
huge as the creatures of pagan myth that warred against
Heaven's King—the Titans and the Giants. These bring
in a certain notion of hideousness as well as of terror, for
Briareüs is the monster with fifty heads and Typhon is
a hundred-headed serpent monster. Not, of course, that

[1] *P.L.* I. 192–210.

Milton is saying that Satan is hideous or hundred-headed, but only that he is as huge as these enormous grotesque figures of ancient fable, the enemies of Jove. He is allowing the thought of their hideousness and the thought of their vast destructive, abortive war against Olympus to enter into the poem and colour our imagination of Satan. And he then proceeds, on the model of older epic poets, to give us a purely extraneous detail that has nothing to do with Satan, a piece of information: that Typhon lived in a den in Cilicia, which he gives us in a curiously roundabout way by telling us that the den was near Tarsus, the ancient capital of Cilicia. This giving to Typhon the monster a local habitation, as well as a name, gives him 'body', as it were, makes him appear less purely fabulous, and allows us a pause in which to take in the names and make them more than names; and we may respond as we wish to the name of Tarsus, birthplace of that Saul who 'laid waste the church' and breathed 'threatening and slaughter against the disciples of the Lord' until he met the Lord on the Damascus road. Then back we come again to 'hugeness', to the natural world and Leviathan 'slumbring on the *Norway* foam' as Satan lies floating on the waves of Hell, and are delighted and refreshed by a traveller's anecdote, an old bestiary theme, again given a local habitation. This gives us a vivid sense of the hugeness of Satan, for it introduces the first of the many human figures in the poem by which Milton reminds us, as Swift so constantly does in *Gulliver's Travels*, of our human sense of scale. The anecdote, though for the moment leading us far from Satan, has its appropriate overtones of night and darkness and of a boat near wrecked, or else to be wrecked. We may take 'night-founder'd' as proleptic if we wish to. And the pilot in his small skiff, anchoring by this vast looming shape in the darkness, hoping he has found safety and longing for the light that seems as if it will never come, has the frailty and the pathos

with which Milton so constantly invests the human
figures that he introduces through his similes into his
poem. The shape is now quiescent as it slumbers, but if
it wakes or even stirs in its sleep it will overwhelm the
pilot and his 'small skiff'. I cannot feel that Milton would
have done better to give us a sharply visualized picture
of Satan instead of thus stimulating in us a play of feeling
before this huge prone figure, who in the next moment

rears from off the Pool
His mighty Stature.

And I think that to complain that Milton's world lacks
sharp outlines is to fail to recognize the nature of his
subject as he conceived it.

　　Milton's conception of his subject is the source of what
has always been regarded as one of the chief glories of
Paradise Lost, its wealth of epic similes. The epic simile—
whether in the form of an extended image, moving off
from a point of comparison and returning to it at the
close, like a balloon moored at both ends; or moving on
to a further point of comparison that arises apparently
naturally as the simile comes to its close; or, as here, a
cluster of allusions—is Milton's grand weapon for con-
veying to us the substance of his epic. In the similes the
detail is often sharp and precise enough, and they supply
much of that 'human interest' which Johnson declared
was missing in *Paradise Lost*. It is true, in one sense, that
the poem has only two human characters, and that they
are in a situation for most of the poem remote from any
situation we could conceivably find ourselves in; but the
poem is full of human beings, their achievements, their
disasters, their fears and hopes, and their everyday concerns. The similes draw on ordinary life and the natural
world we all inhabit. They bring before ūs not merely
monsters of legends and heroes of antiquity, but a pilot
off his course at night, a ploughman anxious for his

harvest, a drunken peasant intruding on fairy revels, a burglar, a young man out for an early morning walk in the fields around a city who catches sight of a pretty girl. In the similes these figures come before us as vividly as figures in the background or seen through windows in great subject paintings: a dog playing on the floor where Christ sits in the house of Simon the Leper, or a serving-girl flirting while she pours out wine at the back, or a child peering inquisitively round a door in a painting of the Annunciation. But beyond the richness of human interest that the similes carry and the brilliance and precision of so much of their detail, the simile exactly solves the great problem of Milton's subject; how to convey imaginatively what 'surmounts the reach of human sense', how to describe without describing and to preserve in us the sense that what he tells us is both true and a fiction. The simile says at the same time 'like' and 'not like'. Or, in the form that Milton made particularly his own, the negative simile, it says 'not like' but yet 'not wholly unlike'. Comparison must always involve both likeness and difference. We can no more compare the identical than the wholly different. The similes perpetually appeal to our memories, to our sense experience, and to our moral experience as well as to our reading; but they ask us not to rest in these. The extensive use that Milton makes of simile is the natural result of his whole conception of his subject. For, *Paradise Lost* considered as a whole is like a vast simile, and asks from us the same kind of response as we give to a simile: that we delight in its beauty and interest and accept that it is like but yet not like the things of which it tells us.

III

THE COSMIC THEME

MILTON's subject is 'the wayes of God to men'. This is the central concern of his poem, the subject that engages him most deeply as a moral being. The great myth of the Adversary of God, through whose guile man was seduced, provides a frame, a comparison, and a contrast to the story of man's creation, fall, and restoration: a frame, because it sets human history within a struggle that began before history and takes place outside, as well as within, history; a comparison, because both angels and men are created in God's image, free to serve him or to disobey, and both choose to disobey; a contrast, because man may find grace and pardon through penitence but the angels are beyond the possibility of grace. Although Milton does not expressly make the point, it was held that one great distinction between angels and men was that men were capable of penitence, could turn back and ask and find pardon, but that angels, once fallen, could not change and were incapable of feeling penitence. One early Father, Origen, the only one as far as I know, held a different view and thought that 'in the end' even Satan might repent and be restored, so that the apostle's vision might be fulfilled and God be 'all in all'. Donne refers to the view of 'this tender Father', but only as a curiosity of Christian thought, not as a view that could be seriously entertained.[1] It is one of the data, things accepted without question, in *Paradise Lost* that the fallen angels are for ever fallen. They

[1] See my article on 'Milton's Satan and the Theme of Damnation', reprinted as Appendix A.

have chosen once and for all to range themselves against God and to attempt to thwart his will. The Satan of *Paradise Lost* declares without reserve, and without contradiction, and that he and his followers are committed

> To wage by force or guile eternal Warr
> Irreconcileable, to our grand Foe.[1]

And in soliloquy he confesses that 'true repentance' is something outside the bounds of his imagination:

> But say I could repent and could obtaine
> By Act of Grace my former state; how soon
> Would highth recal high thoughts, how soon unsay
> What feign'd submission swore: ease would recant
> Vows made in pain, as violent and void.
> For never can true reconcilement grow
> Where wounds of deadly hate have peirc'd so deep.[2]

The most imaginative of French novelists, Balzac, describing Vautrin at bay in *Le Père Goriot*, seized on the Miltonic conception of Satan and his Hell when he saw in the convict 'un poème infernal où se peignirent tous les sentiments humains, moins un seul, celui de repentir', and added: 'Son regard etait celui de l'archange déchu qui veut toujours la guerre'. Satan 'veut toujours la guerre'.

It is the very differently conceived Satan of *Paradise Regained*, the 'disconsolate chimera' that attacks the Word in the desert, who says to the Son

> The Son of God I also am, or was,
> And if I was, I am; relation stands.[3]

In *Paradise Lost* the revolt of Satan has no colour of filial disobedience, and the response of his Creator has in it no element of outraged paternity. The revolt is conceived of wholly in political and military terms, as a rebellion

---

[1] *P.L.* I. 121-2.
[2] *P.L.* IV. 93-99.
[3] *P.R.* IV. 518-19.

E

against the Monarchy of Heaven.[1] It is treated by Heaven's Monarch as a rebellion to be crushed, or rather to be first defeated and then 'contained'. The rebels are not to be destroyed; they are to be left free to continue the war by what means they can employ. They can even indulge in the illusion that they are creating a rival empire and achieving 'co-existence'. But all their activity is to be frustrated in the end, though they are to be allowed considerable partial and local successes. They are to be punished and humiliated from time to time. At other times their pains appear to be negligible, and they may enjoy the illusion of power.

The myth of the revolt of the angels does nothing to explain the origin of evil or to solve the metaphysical problem of the existence of evil in a world created and ruled by a good God. Why beings 'sufficient to have stood', natives of Heaven, chose to fall, how Sin was born in Heaven itself—if there is any answer to such questions it is not to be found in *Paradise Lost*. Both myth and poem present to us an image of reality: that there exists in the universe as we know it and in eternity a permanent, irreconcileable hostility between a will to good and a will to evil. These two contrary energies are displayed in the centre of Milton's epic. In the story of the revolt of the angels and the War in Heaven we are shown energy directed to destruction for the sake of personal aggrandisement. In the story of how the world we inhabit came into being we are shown energy directed to creation, to the bringing into existence of manifold, independent forms of life, which will enjoy their own being freely. Milton profoundly believes that the will to evil is overruled, that the will to good is the final will in the universe. In the end

[1] As Bagehot said: 'We seem to be reading about some emperor of history, who admits his son to a share in the empire, who confers on him a considerable jurisdiction, and requires officials, with "Standards and gonfalons", to bow before him' (*Literary Studies*, 1910, ii. 206–7).

> Evil on it self shall back recoyl,
> And mix no more with goodness, when at last
> Gather'd like scum, and setl'd to it self
> It shall be in eternal restless change
> Self-fed and self-consum'd.[1]

This was Milton's faith when he wrote *Comus*. It remains his faith in *Paradise Lost*. Evil will never become converted into good, and it is indestructible. It will neither be absorbed into good, nor melt away like snow in sunshine. But ultimately it cannot harm. The will to destroy calls forth the contrary energies of goodness, which is more powerful to restore than evil is to damage. Goodness will in the end expel evil into outer darkness, creating

> New Heav'ns, new Earth, Ages of endless date
> Founded in righteousness and peace and love,
> To bring forth fruits Joy and eternal Bliss.[2]

It is impossible to deny that Milton's presentation of the Adversary and of Hell is far more impressive than his presentation of God and Heaven. One reason why he 'wrote in fetters' when he wrote of Heaven is that there exist in Scripture images and fictions to describe Heaven which his own theory of Scripture told him were chosen by God to illuminate our understanding. His chief poetic instrument, the simile, he does not use to make Heaven vivid to our imagination. The Book of Revelation is the great obstacle. Its oriental imagery and exotic symbolism prevented him from exercising his own power to suggest. He at times hints, being a true son of Plato, that all that we enjoy on earth, even the grateful change of day to night

---

[1] *Comus*, ll. 593–6.

[2] *P.L.* XII. 549–51. In the immediately preceding lines Milton does say that at the Second Coming Christ will 'dissolve *Satan* with his perverted world'; but in view of the unambiguous statement in the *De Doctrina Christiana* (Book I, chapter vii) that 'no created thing can finally be annihilated' we must take it that it is Satan's lordship over the world that will be dissolved, not that he himself will return to non-being.

and night to day, not to mention the delight that lovers have in each other, is enjoyed in Heaven. But he only too often succeeds in suggesting, most un-Platonically, that Heaven is a rather poor copy of earth, not the ideal of which all earth's beauty is only a shadow. Satan, who had after all been in Heaven, though perhaps his fall had impaired his memory and judgement, thinks earth might 'more justly' be 'preferr'd' than compared to Heaven;[1] and we have to own that Milton's Heaven, perfunctorily described,[2] cannot with his 'Paradise of *Eden* strive'. There is a defect here in the poem; but I cannot feel it is serious. It is analogous to the disappointment that we feel when looking at some great religious paintings, where the whole design points to a central theophany that is handled conventionally, and even lamely, whereas all the elements in the composition of which it is the centre are handled with originality and vigour. The only banal object in Van Eyck's *Adoration of the Lamb* is the Lamb. It might have been the work of any sign-painter. This does not hinder our enjoyment of the whole composition and the variety and beauty of all that surrounds the central conventional symbol.

More serious than the conventional treatment of the joys and occupations of Heaven is the presentation of the Father and of 'Heav'ns high Councel-Table'. There is a fundamental absurdity in making a God a theologian. As Bagehot observed: 'If you once attribute reasoning to Him, subsequent logicians may discover that He does not reason very well.' But deeper than this objection is the revulsion that many readers feel at the presentation of God as Monarch of Heaven rather than as the Father of angels as well as of men, whose 'nature and whose Name is Love'. The face that God turns towards Satan and his followers is the face of immutable Law vainly defied and

[1] *P.L.* IX. 99–101.
[2] See *P.L.* III. 345–71 and v. 616–54.

of Omnipotence that cannot be shaken. Satan himself, in his soliloquy on Mount Niphates,[1] speaks of 'Heav'ns free Love dealt equally to all', and blasphemously cries 'Be then his Love accurst'. But this is the only suggestion in the poem that Satan is a creature who has rejected Love and found that Love rejected is Wrath. William Law taught that there was no Wrath in God either to the fallen angels or to fallen man: that God was all Love and Light, and that the wrath so constantly spoken of in Scripture was in fallen creatures, not in their Creator, a dark fire springing from the energies of their natures divorced from union with God. Charles Williams, who greatly admired Law's mystical writings, attempted to read this doctrine into *Paradise Lost*,[2] and to defend the 'irrepressible laughter of Heaven' at the 'solemn antics' of Satan with the statement 'Love laughs at anti-love'. I cannot feel that this is anything but an anachronism and a forcing of Milton's text. Milton fully accepts the Scriptural ascription of Wrath to offended Deity, and, since he conceives of Satan's revolt in purely political terms his God is, as far as Satan is concerned, simply a stronger power, the All-Ruler. We cannot say: 'This is how God appears to Satan who has chosen to cut himself off from Light and Love and so sees only Fire and Wrath.' This is how God appears to us, as far as Satan is concerned: implacable, vengeful, and deriding. The implacability of God towards his revolted subjects is, in the whole design of the poem, the background that frames his mercy to his disobedient children. The cosmic theme is the war of Good and Evil, and it is on both sides *à l'outrance*.

In writing of Hell and Satan Milton's imagination was 'unfettered'. Apart from 'adamantine chains and penal fire', 'outer darkness', and 'weeping and gnashing of teeth', there is little to create an image of Hell in Scripture, and

---

[1] *P.L.* IV. 32–113.

[2] See the Introduction to *The English Poems of Milton* (World's Classics), 1940.

the references to Satan and to devils are scattered, ambiguous, and poetically suggestive.[1] There was, of course, much in tradition; but Milton was free to accept or reject traditions. His imagination was here at liberty to invent and virtually to create. It was at liberty also, I would suggest, because his deepest religious feelings and beliefs were not engaged. He could here address himself, in Sir Kenneth Clark's words, 'to the connoisseur'. Accepting, and legitimately expecting that his readers would accept, the implacable hostility of God and Satan, Good and Evil, Light and Dark, his imagination was liberated to make every aspect of the contest as dramatic and expressive as he could, and to make the figure of the Great Adversary as thrilling and as 'noble' as the subject allowed. I say 'as the subject allowed' because the strength of Milton's presentation of Satan lies in the fact that he does not have to prove to his readers that Satan is wicked, or persuade them that this is their 'Grand Foe', the 'Enemy of Mankind'. As the whole poem swings between two uses of the word 'Providence', so the presentation of Satan begins and ends with the same word and image:

> Who first seduc'd them to that fowl revolt?
> Th' infernal Serpent; he it was . . .;

and our last vision of Satan is as

> A monstrous serpent on his belly prone.

That is Satan's fundamental role in the poem, and we are never allowed to forget that the aim of all his activity is

> To wreak on innocent frail man his loss.

But having introduced Satan as 'the infernal Serpent', Milton immediately begins his characteristic expansive

---

[1] Texts referring to evil angels are collected together in three short paragraphs in the *De Doctrina Christiana* (Book I, chapter ix).

movement and at once sets before us the splendid ambiguity of Satan's role as tempter of man and adversary of
God.

> Th' infernal Serpent; he it was, whose guile
> Stird up with Envy and Revenge, deceiv'd
> The Mother of Mankinde, what time his Pride
> Had cast him out from Heav'n, with all his Host
> Of Rebel Angels, by whose aid aspiring
> To set himself in Glory above his Peers,
> He trusted to have equal'd the most High,
> If he oppos'd; and with ambitious aim
> Against the Throne and Monarchy of God
> Rais'd impious War in Heav'n and Battel proud
> With vain attempt.[1]

He is the *infernal Serpent* who acted by *guile*, the coward's
way, and he was stirred up by *Envy*, the basest and most
despicable, the meanest and the most ignoble, of the seven
deadly sins; but he was also stirred up by *Revenge*—and
here we begin to be moved, because revenge is an old
heroic motive, a motive that inspired the great heroes of
primitive epic and saga. And from the thought of revenge
we come to *Pride*, the deadliest of the seven deadly sins
the theologians tell us; but to our unregenerate imaginations, pride is a sin that is very near a virtue, and certainly
does not call forth contempt. The infernal serpent, con-
sumed with bitter envy, has begun to fade into the proud
leader of a *Host of Rebel Angels*. But what was the aim of
the revolt? *To set himself in Glory above his Peers*. This is
not the heroic leader of a band of brothers fighting for
liberty and just rights; but a great adventurer, thirsting
for personal dominion and glory. But here again, the
desire for fame and glory, though an infirmity, is 'an infirmity of noble mind', and to have trusted *to have equalled
the most High* is not a meanly *ambitious aim*. And ambition,

[1] *P.L.* I. 34-44.

like pride, is an ambiguous word, condemned by the moral theologian but not always in our common usage.[1] Satan's ambitious aim *raised impious War in Heav'n*, and this seems the height of horror, that there should be War in Heaven, with Satan 'Warring in Heav'n against Heav'ns matchless King'; but the War in Heaven was *Battel proud*. Though impious, it was still glorious. Satan comes before us invested with the grandeur of 'Battle's magnificently stern array', the 'Pride, pomp and circumstance of glorious war'. But though glorious, it was with *vain attempt*. It was supremely foolish.

Milton thus at the beginning of the poem gives us in outline the base, the heroic, the awful, the splendid, the insanely presumptuous figure of 'Him . . . who durst defie th' Omnipotent to Arms'. The greatest of English critics, Coleridge, saw at once the true analogy for Satan in the great conquerors of history:

The character of Satan is pride and sensual indulgence, finding in self the sole motive of action. It is the character so often seen *in little* on the political stage. It exhibits all the restlessness, temerity, and cunning which have marked the mighty hunters of mankind from Nimrod to Napoleon. The common fascination of men is, that these great men, as they are called, must act from some great motive. Milton has carefully marked in his Satan the intense selfishness, the alcohol of egotism, which would rather reign in hell than serve in heaven. To place this lust of self in opposition to denial of self or duty, and to show what exertions it would make, and what pains endure to accomplish its end, is Milton's particular object in the character of Satan. But around this character he has thrown a singularity of daring, a grandeur of sufferance, and a ruined splendour, which constitute the very height of poetic sublimity.[2]

This height of poetic sublimity is achieved in Satan's first speech, perhaps the greatest expression in our literature

[1] Thus we speak in common parlance of a 'proper' or 'just' pride, when we should never so qualify envy, and to say of someone that he has 'no ambition' may more often mean blame than praise.

[2] *Miscellaneous Criticism*, edited by Raysor, 1936, p. 163.

of a virtue that must always command awe and admiration: fortitude in adversity, courage when there is no longer hope. Milton does not hesitate to allow to Satan a full measure of the grandest of all virtues, courage or perseverance, the root virtue without which no other virtue can flourish. That it is courage and perseverance in a bad cause, a kind of madness, does not make it any the less courage. The fighting man who

> when his legs were smitten off
> He fought upon his stumps,

or the young artillery officer on Singapore airport who went on firing as long as he had ammunition to fire with, long after all hope of reinforcement had gone, de Gaulle, with his few followers in 1940, asserting in defiance of what seemed total defeat 'All is not lost'—such actions are glorious in themselves, irrespective of the rights or wrongs of the cause in question. As Keats wrote

> Though a quarrel in the Streets is a thing to be hated, the energies displayed in it are fine; the commonest Man shows a grace in his quarrel—By a superior being our reasonings may take the same tone—though erroneous they may be fine—This is the very thing in which consists poetry.[1]

So Satan's archangelic strength and resolution are 'fine', and the taunts by which he arouses his dispirited followers, culminating in the superb

> Awake, arise, or be for ever fallen

must always arouse the thrilled response that supreme courage evokes.[2]

[1] *Letters*, edited by M. Buxton Forman, second edition, 1935, p. 317.
[2] Bagehot, commenting on Coleridge's comparison of Satan with Napoleon, says of the adventure of the Hundred Days: 'Our opinion is against him, our serious wish is of course for England; but the imagination has a sympathy of its own, and will not give place.' It is this 'sympathy of its own' that some modern criticisms of *Paradise Lost* seem to refuse to allow to our imaginations.

Milton could afford to present Satan grandly, and allow us to admire his virtues, because he is doomed. We know from the beginning that he must fail. If we were allowed to think for a moment that Satan might succeed, our feelings would be different; and Milton's treatment would have had to be different too, if he could not rely upon our recognition throughout that Satan is our 'Grand Foe' as well as God's. He can give him all the splendour and tragic beauty of an archangel ruined, as he can make him the most beautiful of all serpents. He can put into his mouth the most seductive and impassioned arguments, eloquently shaped and phrased as if by 'som Oratour renound in *Athens* or free *Rome*'. He need deny him no gifts, except the one gift: the power to love, that is to wish good to another being than himself.

Milton's treatment of Satan has all the ambiguity of the Christian attitude to sin and evil. Sin, say the speculative theologians, is 'nothing', it is non-existent, a privation of good; it has no ultimate reality, only goodness is real. Sin, say the moral theologians, is an awful reality, cutting man off from God and from his true life in God.[1] Its wages is death. So Satan is both the fool who absurdly thinks he can stand against God, when all he does is by God's permission, and whose malice only serves to bring forth more goodness, more glory to God, and more good will towards men; and Satan is terrible and dangerous, the author of 'all our woe', the perverter of the goodness and beauty of the universe who shook God's throne and brought Sin and Death to ravage his creation. The same ambiguity underlies Milton's treatment of God as Satan's adversary and accounts for some of the discomfort this causes. No Christian looking at the world and at history can deny that evil flourishes and triumphs again and again. No Christian can believe that evil will ultimately triumph,

---

[1] Cf. the paradox with which Donne ends his 'Litany':
As sinne is nothing, let it no where be.

that good and evil are equally poised. Milton's presentation of the King of Heaven attempts to combine the sense that the war is desperately serious with the sense that it is not: that Satan is a dangerous foe, capable of damaging the peace and beauty of Heaven itself, and that Satan's enterprise is futile, since, though he creates havoc and ruin, when the moment comes he will be cast out, leaving behind him no trace of the ruin he has caused, Heaven being Heaven still. What Professor Empson has called God's 'blood-curdling jokes' arise from a fundamental necessary equivocation in Milton's treatment of Satan's revolt and of the War in Heaven.

Many critics since Johnson have complained of the unreality of the War in Heaven. Even when it has been explained to us by the historical scholars that the concept of angelic corporeality was not Milton's invention but was seriously entertained in his day,[1] the difficulties remain. By the standards of modern science fiction the whole affair lacks imaginative consistency. If angels can change shape at will, contract or enlarge their dimensions, and cannot receive any wound that does not immediately heal, it seems unnecessary for them to wear armour and extremely odd that this armour, whatever it is made of, should impede them. Milton, through the mouth of Raphael, provides a double defence. The archangel declares that he will tell the story in terms that do not 'surmount the reach of human sense' by 'lik'ning spiritual to corporal forms, as may express them best'; but he then characteristically confuses us by hinting that perhaps Heaven is more like earth than we think. Milton thus leaves us free to give what credence we choose to his narrative. It is an example on a grand scale of his 'like but not like'. The angels themselves, though capable of infinite shape-changing and gifted with powers that make

---

[1] See C. S. Lewis, *Preface to 'Paradise Lost'*, 1942, chapter xv, 'The Mistake about Milton's Angels'.

them quite unlike us, have yet, it seems, a 'native form', or 'proper form'—the form in which Satan springs up at the touch of Ithuriel's spear when discovered

> Squat like a Toad, close at the eare of *Eve*,[1]

or the form that Raphael reassumes on landing on earth after winging his way down through the spheres as a glorious bird.[2] This native form, as in all great art, is a glorified human body, sometimes winged, sometimes apparently without wings. The War in Heaven can thus be like and unlike wars on earth, and can both present in symbolic form the conflict of good and evil outside history and provide an epitome of, and comment on, the wars of history.

Milton himself said that he was

> Not sedulous by Nature to indite
> Warrs, hitherto the onely Argument
> Heroic deem'd,[3]

and in Book XII, in Michael's reply to Adam's inquiry as to how the Son will bruise the Serpent's head, he in his own fashion warns us that the story of the War in Heaven is extraneous, in a sense, to the true theme and central concerns of his poem.

>   Dream not of thir fight
> As of a Duel, or the local wounds
> Of head or heel: not therefore joynes the Son
> Manhood to God-head, with more strength to foil
> Thy enemie; nor so is overcome
> *Satan*, whose fall from Heav'n, a deadlier bruise,
> Disabl'd not to give thee thy deaths wound:
> Which hee, who comes thy Saviour, shall recure,
> Not by destroying *Satan*, but his works
> In thee and in thy Seed.[4]

[1] *P.L.* IV. 799–819.   [2] *P.L.* V. 266–85.
[3] *P.L.* IX. 27–29.   [4] *P.L.* XII. 386–95.

All the same, he could not omit this episode. Without the defiance of Abdiel and the fight between Michael and Satan, the poem would have no counterpoise to the heroic treatment of Satan's enterprise in the first two books. Although Milton believed in the superiority of his true subject, 'the better fortitude of Patience and Heroic Martyrdom', to the subjects of ancient epic, he dared not leave all the active and traditionally heroic virtues to Satan. The story makes it impossible for the good angels to play impressive roles. As sentries they are more ornamental than useful. They cannot be allowed to catch Satan or keep him permanently out of Paradise. He must find his way in, in spite of their watch and ward. They must, if the story is to go on, fall down on their job. It is difficult to imagine a less heroic situation than that of the 'Angelic Guards' at the opening of Book X, when they ascend 'mute and sad' to Heaven,

> Much wondring how the suttle Fiend had stoln
> Entrance unseen,

inform the citizens of Heaven of the 'unwelcome news', and hasten to the 'Throne Supream' to explain that they really had done their utmost, and are graciously excused for their failure. The War in Heaven allows Milton to present the servants of God as mightier as well as more beautiful than his foes. Further, Milton wanted his epic to surpass all other epics, to give all they gave and more. He could not wholly reject what his great predecessors had lavished their art upon, the clash of armies and the combats of champions, and leave the old heroic virtues unhonoured and unsung.

No other part of the story allowed him to show the freedom that God by creation gave to angels and men exercised both ways. Nothing is more justly admired in the whole of *Paradise Lost* than the scene that is the prelude to the war. Satan's political oration was compared by

Charles Williams to the speech by which Antony inflames
the Roman mob against the 'honourable men' who murdered Caesar:

> Thrones, Dominations, Princedomes, Vertues, Powers,
> If these magnific Titles yet remain
> Not meerly titular, since by Decree
> Another now hath to himself ingross't
> All Power, and us eclipst under the name
> Of King anointed, for whom all this haste
> Of midnight march, and hurried meeting here,
> This only to consult how we may best
> With what may be devised of honours new
> Receive him coming to receive from us
> Knee-tribute yet unpaid, prostration vile,
> Too much to one, but double how endur'd
> To one and to his image now proclaim'd?[1]

Its irony, sarcasm, and final direct appeal to the Lords of
Heaven to 'cast off this Yoke' are answered by the fervent
zeal of Abdiel. Milton's imagination always responds to
the image of the 'one just man', the solitary champion of
right, and it is a noble image; but this scene has another
purpose beside that of celebrating the glory of lonely
fidelity, though this it most splendidly does:

> So spake the Seraph *Abdiel* faithful found,
> Among the faithless, faithful only hee;
> Among innumerable false, unmov'd,
> Unshak'n, unseduc'd, unterrifi'd
> His Loyaltie he kept, his Love, his Zeale;
> Nor number, nor example with him wrought
> To swerve from truth, or change his constant mind
> Though single.[2]

Sin to Milton is not a disposition of the mind but an act,
and an act of deliberate choice. The angels who have followed Satan, as Abdiel has, to 'the Quarters of the North'
have not sinned by doing so. Nor do they sin by listening

[1] *P.L.* v. 769–81.   [2] *P.L.* v. 893–900.

to Satan. The way back is open to them still. They may reject Satan's arguments and remain the sinless servants of God. As Raphael's narrative is to make the sin of Adam and Eve 'inexcusable', by giving them every warning, so Abdiel's speech makes the sin of the other angels deliberate. They choose to remain with Satan, and Abdiel alone turns back. His return is the sole and supreme image in the poem of contrary choice, of the will to obey, to reject evil and choose good.

> All night the dreadless Angel unpursu'd
> Through Heav'ns wide Champain held his way. . . .[1]

The War in Heaven itself is to be read as a fiction or parable shadowing truths. A war between immortals who can neither die nor be seriously injured is a curious kind of war, and it is difficult to take seriously a campaign in which the full force of either side is limited by the 'Eternal King Omnipotent', and in which the doom of the rebel angels is suspended to make the two sides a better match. The episode as a whole is more like a vast tournament than a war, and it goes on just as long as the ruler of the lists allows. But for Messiah's intervention it would have been endless. It becomes thus a parable of the war of good and evil as long as the world lasts, a struggle in which good, though tested to the uttermost, cannot be overcome, but also cannot overcome. The triumph of the good waits for the moment when Messiah will appear on the clouds at the Last Day. The expulsion of Satan and his followers from Heaven is conceived of as Michelangelo conceived of the Last Judgement: *Christus Victor* casting down forever his enemies. The war also provides an epitome of the wars of history; and the mounting horror and destructiveness of the battles corresponds with Milton's sense of the deepening tragedy of human history, so poignantly expressed in the last books of *Paradise Lost*. The war that begins

[1] *P.L.* VI. 1–2.

with 'pride, pomp and circumstance' and images of heroism ends with horrible indignity and senseless destruction. The narrative itself provides the justification for Milton's rejection of war, heroic or chivalric, as the argument of a poem that was to be doctrinal to his own age and to ages to come. At its close, in the utter confusion and havoc with which what began with such dignity ends, the War in Heaven suddenly sharply touches our imagination.

Milton begins with the old heroic defiance of champions, each advancing into the 'narrow space' between 'Host and Host'. And after their speeches of defiance we have the single combat of Satan and Abdiel. There follows the general engagement, with chariot charges on either side, in which each individual warrior seemed himself a 'Leader' or 'Chief'. This culminates in the single combat of Satan and Michael, after which Satan is wounded and borne off the field by a rescuing band of his followers. The good angels stand their ground

> In Cubic Phalanx firm advanc't, entire,
> Invulnerable, impenitrably arm'd:
> Such high advantages thir innocence
> Gave them above thir foes, not to have sinn'd,
> Not to have disobei'd.[1]

The phalanx order in battle, with shields overlapping, was one of the great advances in the art of war in antiquity. It here provides Milton with a fine image of unshakeable dignity and strength in the confusion and turmoil of the battle, 'as those smaller squares in battell unite in one great cube, the main phalanx, an embleme of truth and stedfastnesse'.[2]

Night falls with Michael and his host in possession of the field; but during the night Satan and his followers invent gunpowder. The invention of gunpowder was

---

[1] *P.L.* VI. 399–403.   [2] *Reason of Church Government*, Book I, chapter vi.

Michelangelo: Detail from The Last Judgement (Sistine Chapel)

ascribed to the devil long before Milton. Both Spenser, and Ariosto before him, regarded cannon as a

> diuelish yron Engin wrought
> In deepest Hell, and framd by *Furies* skill.[1]

In the ninth canto of the *Orlando Furioso* there is a description of a hideous engine which the King of Friesland employs against the King of Holland's daughter:

> No doubt some fiend of hell or divellish wight
> Devised it to do mankind a spite.[2]

It is

> A weapon vile, wherwith a foolish boy
> May worthy Captaines mischiefe and annoy.[2]

In other words, it is a cannon, which no amount of individual heroic prowess can withstand, the great destroyer of chivalry and chivalrous exploits. Orlando, when he has defeated the King of Friesland and captured his engine, throws it into the sea:

> Because (said he) hereafter never more
> May any Knight of life and limb be reft
> By thee, or coward vaunt him with the stout.[2]

It is a

> curst device found out by some foule fend,
> And fram'd below by *Belzebub* in hell,
> Who by thy meane did purpose and intend,
> To ruine all that on the earth do dwell.[2]

---

[1] *Faerie Queene*, I. vii. 13.

[2] Quotations are from Harington's translation. The first two are additions by Harington, but the last two render Ariosto fairly closely:

> Acciò più non istea
> mai cavallier per te d'essere ardito,
> né quanto il buono val, mai più si vanti
> il rio per te valer, qui giù rimanti.

> O maladetto, o abominoso ordigno,
> che fabricato nel tartareo fondo
> fosti per man di Belzebù maligno
> che ruinar per te disegnò il mondo,
> all'inferno, onde uscisti, ti rasigno.

Orlando regards it as a vilely ungentlemanly weapon,
levelling the brave man with the coward and the strong
with the weak. Milton is following tradition in giving the
invention of this terrible destructive force to his devils.
He insists on the fraud and treachery with which they
use it, and, like Ariosto, he sees it as depriving war of any
dignity and warriors of their prowess. It renders the good
angels ludicrous, as they roll on their backs impeded by
their armour. The war becomes a hideous farce. The good
angels recover, and find an answer by tearing up the hills
of Heaven. Their enemies retaliate in kind.

> Warr seem'd a civil Game
> To this uproar; horrid confusion heapt
> Upon confusion rose.

It is here that the War in Heaven touches us home who
have seen whole cities devastated and fear yet more whole-
sale destructions. The Almighty declares

> Warr wearied hath perform'd what Warr can do,
> And to disorder'd rage let loose the reines,
> With Mountains as with Weapons arm'd, which makes
> Wild work in Heav'n, and dangerous to the maine.

He intervenes not to protect his own forces but to bring
the whole business to an end. The appearance of the Son
in Majesty restores the ruins of Heaven, and the terror
of his countenance drives the rebels before him. They are
not destroyed. They are rooted out of Heaven. God is
Creator and cannot destroy what he has created, for that
would be a contradiction of his essential being. The gift of
life and freedom cannot be revoked. If it could, it would
not be a gift.

The War in Heaven shows Milton's virtuosity in one
way: his skill in adapting to his own theme and purpose
a traditional element in ancient epic that had ceased to
hold serious meaning for his age. The narrative of the
Creation that follows shows it in another way. It is central

to his theme and subject, and he marks its importance by a special prologue. He was heir to a long tradition of comment on the work of the six days; no book of the Bible had received more, or more extensive, commentary than the book which told how the world came into being. Milton's task as an artist was to make exquisite variations on a classic theme, to rival and surpass the most famous and popular poem of the first half of the seventeenth century, Sylvester's translation of Du Bartas, *The Divine Weeks and Works*. Years before, in the 'Vacation Exercise', Milton as a young man of nineteen had revealed his desire to

> sing of secret things that came to pass
> When Beldam Nature in her cradle was;

and six years later, in *Comus*, he had put into the mouth of Comus wonderful lines on the bounty, fertility, and delicacy of Nature, who pours her bounties forth

> With such a full and unwithdrawing hand
> Covering the earth with odours, fruits and flocks,
> Thronging the Seas with spawn innumerable,

and who sets to work

> millions of spinning Worms
> That in their green shops weave the smooth-hair'd silk
> To deck her Sons.

When he came to set against the destructive activity of Satan the creative activity of the Son, Milton combined in the same way a sense of the immense, overflowing abundance of the creation with a sense of its marvellous, exquisite variety. And while he included a mass of scientific theory and explanation, he kept the whole moving as narrative. We see not only the 'stately Trees' rising 'as in Dance', but the whole world coming into being as in a ballet, with the stage at first dim and empty, then gradually lightening and filling up, until at the end the whole is brilliantly lit and alive with moving figures, each performing its own graceful or vigorous part in the whole.

We begin with acts of limitation and separation, the initial acts by which the universe is distinguished from chaos and its bounds set. As the King of Glory

in his powerful Word
And Spirit coming to create new Worlds

passes through the Gates of Heaven, he looks out upon 'the vast immeasurable Abyss'

Outrageous as a Sea, dark, wasteful, wilde,
Up from the bottom turn'd by furious windes
And surging waves, as Mountains to assault
Heav'ns highth, and with the Center mix the Pole.[1]

This chaos has to be ordered 'by measure, and number and weight';[2] but first it must be stilled by the same word of power by which the wind was rebuked and the sea calmed on the Lake of Galilee:[3]

Silence, ye troubled waves, and thou Deep, peace.

Far out in Chaos, the Creator stays his chariot and takes the golden Compasses in his hand. The compass is a great traditional symbol of reason and order, by which bounds are set and all things disposed in right proportion. Geometry, among the Liberal Arts, is always seen with compasses, and Geometry was the science *par excellence* for early Renaissance artists. In miniatures God the Father and Creator is frequently shown with compasses, and sometimes compasses and scales, as architect of the world, as in Durer's *Melencolia I* creative genius is shown with the compasses in her right hand.[4] The work of the first

[1] *P.L.* VII. 212–15.

[2] As the Neoplatonist author of the Wisdom of Solomon wrote: 'But by measure and number and weight thou didst order all things' (xi. 20).

[3] 'And he awoke and rebuked the wind, and said unto the sea, Peace, be still' (Mark iv. 39).

[4] See Klibansky, Saxl, and Panovsky, *Saturn and Melancholy*, 1964, p. 339.

two days is the work of the great Architect, or Builder
of the universe. But, as soon as he comes to the division
of land and sea, Milton's imagination begins to luxuriate,
and the Creator is no longer a great Workmaster, planning, regulating, and ordering, but a Giver of Life, calling
into being things instinct with the spirit of life that hasten,
as if endowed before with powers and wills of their own,
to come into existence and take their place in the whole
dance: the mountains heaving their 'broad bare backs' into
the clouds, the waters hastening 'with glad precipitance'.
This sense of everything enjoying its being, the sun
'jocund to run his Longitude', the Pleiades dancing before
him, comes to a climax in the work of the fifth and sixth
days, the days of the creation of fish and fowl and of
beasts. Milton conveys here the essence of what he means
by creation: the liberation of energies of every kind har-
moniously disposed. His whole style and manner, instinct
with gaiety, renders his sense of the fullness of the natural
world and of its order, as in the beautiful variation he makes
on the words 'And God created the great sea-monsters,
and every living creature that moveth, which the waters
brought forth abundantly, after their kinds':

> Forthwith the Sounds and Seas, each Creek & Bay
> With Frie innumerable swarme, and Shoales
> Of Fish that with thir Finns & shining Scales
> Glide under the green Wave, in Sculles that oft
> Bank the mid Sea: part single or with mate
> Graze the Sea weed thir pasture, & through Groves
> Of Coral stray, or sporting with quick glance
> Show to the Sun thir wav'd coats dropt with Gold,
> Or in thir Pearlie shells at ease, attend
> Moist nutriment, or under Rocks thir food
> In jointed Armour watch: on smooth the Seale,
> And bended Dolphins play: part huge of bulk
> Wallowing unweildie, enormous in thir Gate
> Tempest the Ocean: there Leviathan

> Hugest of living Creatures, on the Deep
> Stretcht like a Promontorie sleeps or swimmes,
> And seems a moving Land, and at his Gilles
> Draws in, and at his Trunck spouts out a Sea.[1]

It makes one feel that it must be fun to be fish; but the whole is organized to give rational delight as a series of contrasts. Both the narrow *Sounds* and the wide *Seas*, winding close *Creek* and smiling open *Bay*, swarm *with Frie innumerable*. The fish with *Finns and shining Scales* flicker glimmering under the *Green Wave*, or, heaped in *Sculles*, or shoals, are like a bank on the surface of the ocean. Some, with only one mate, or more adventurously alone, explore the ocean bed to *graze the Sea weed thir pasture*, or stray through *Groves of Coral*. Others dart about on the surface, while, in contrast, the lazy oysters in their *Pearlie Shells attend moist nutriment*, and the crabs and lobsters in *jointed Armour* stalk their prey. The *Seals* and *Dolphins* play on the calm seas, while the *enormous Leviathan*, lumbering and *unweildie*, creates a tempest as he wallows. For this is before the Fall, and there are no storms except what the great sea-monsters create for their sport.

Milton treats the universe as it comes into being under his pen as inexhaustibly lovely and interesting, but also as intelligible to rational minds. He is inspired by a very ancient conception, stemming from the *Timaeus*: that the goodness of the Creator was displayed in the variety of his creation. Goodness could not be envious or grudging and could therefore not refuse life to any form of being that the mind could conceive. Since this was so, there were no gaps in creation; the species shaded into one another and all was order and degree. Milton adds to these intellectual concepts his own peculiar vitality, which makes the creatures seem to participate in their own birth and struggle to be born before they are. It is proper that he

[1] *P.L.* VII. 399–416.

celebrates the variety and order of the created world by a varied consort of music in Heaven. The Creator is praised by Harp and Pipe and Dulcimer, by Flute and Oboe ('Organs of sweet stop'), by Lutes and Viols ('sounds on Fret by String or Golden Wire') and the voices of angels in solo and in chorus as the Host of Heaven declares that

to create
Is greater then created to destroy.

The seventh is the one purely happy book of *Paradise Lost* and shows Milton's genius at its most genial and delightful, filling out the bare narrative of Genesis with a wealth of knowledge and imagination, with constant touches of observation, of beauty, humour, delicacy, and grotesqueness. It is inspired by Milton's passionate belief in the goodness of the natural world as it was created and his delight in the principle of life, in all its manifestations.

IV

THE HUMAN THEME

THE central subject of *Paradise Lost*, as its title makes clear, is the loss of Eden, or 'Adam Unparadised'. Milton has here to make vivid to us, as Professor Kermode has put it, 'the contrast between what we can imagine as human, and what is so here and now'.[1] Instead of soaring above the Poles and stimulating us to attempt to imagine things that are strictly speaking unimaginable, he has to stand on earth and satisfy our imagination of what I suppose every human being at times imagines, a life in which happiness and joy are free from the infection of sin and guilt and the threat of change, and which is not lived under the shadow of death. He has also to appeal to our experience of life as we know it and as we live it, menaced by sickness, the decay of our minds and bodies, and by mortality, made bitter by the harm we do to others as well as to ourselves, and made joyless by our incapacity for love.

In his handling of his cosmic theme, and particularly in the treatment of Satan as Adversary of God, Milton used all his powers as a heroic poet to invest Satan, as Coleridge said, with 'a ruined splendour' which is 'the very height of poetic sublimity'. The doomed, obstinate figure of Satan, persisting with such energy and fortitude and disdain of pain and such a 'singularity of daring' in his destructive and self-destructive course, has the grandeur of the tragic, the exceptional, the thing that is greater than we are. By contrast, in Adam and Eve,

[1] 'Adam Unparadised', *The Living Milton*, edited by Frank Kermode, 1960, p. 100.

Milton presents us with the ideal and the typical: first, the perfection of our human nature as we may imagine it, and as certain great artists have embodied it in smiling and serene nude figures, then the reality of man in history, sinning, repenting, finding pardon, and walking by faith. The fortitude they display at the close is 'the better fortitude of Patience and Heroic Martyrdom', as they go out into the world, with Providence their guide, to begin the long adventure of human history. It is here that Milton, in Sir Kenneth Clark's words, 'speaks to the believer': in his presentation of the fundamental simplicities of the religious experience of mankind. At the beginning Adam and Eve are ideals which we may cherish but never emulate; at the close they are our models, types of those righteous who will find the 'Paradise within' and enter finally the 'blest Kingdoms meek of joy and love'. Milton showed great daring in including within the scope of a single poem both the thrilling figure of Satan and these two human figures who arouse so different a response. He has dared to mingle the tragic with the ideal or exemplary, the heroic with the human. I imagine there will always be readers for whom the greatness of *Paradise Lost* lies in the cosmic rather than the human, or historic, theme; and others who feel, as I once felt, that in developing the cosmic theme with such power Milton sacrificed the unity of his poem. But I have come to feel the strength of the total design and to see the cosmic theme as framing and interpreting the human theme. The myth of the war of Good and Evil, while it gives grandeur and mystery to the historic theme of man's fall, recedes into the background as we read on and is subordinated to the presentation of man and woman in their relation to each other and to God.

I call the theme of man's fall 'historic', since to Milton and his age Adam and Eve are historic figures and the Paradise they inhabit and are expelled from is an actual

localized garden. Though idealized, it is within the world
of nature as we know it. The 'shifting phantasmagoria',
as Eliot calls it, of Hell and the great Deep beyond surrounds it; but in Paradise itself the time is the time of the
sun, meal-times come round regularly and the time for
sleep and waking, and the garden demands, like our own
gardens, hard work if it is not to become overgrown. But
it is the world as we know it with all that makes that world
unsatisfying removed, the world as it might be 'if we were
things born not to shed a tear'. Although in earlier ages
there had been dispute as to whether Paradise was to be
interpreted allegorically as either the whole world before
the Fall, or as the state of sinless man, and later, when it
had been agreed that it was to be interpreted literally as
an actual region of the earth, there had been argument as
to where it was situated, by the time Milton came to write
it was universally agreed by Catholics and Protestants
alike that the Garden of Eden was a real garden and was in
Mesopotamia. Accepting this geographical location, Milton lavishes all his art on making delightful to the senses
this secret garden of God, high on its mount overlooking
the region of Eden. Like all gardens of romance it is
walled and has a gate, and it is surrounded by steep forests.
The great river of Eden flows under the Mount of Paradise and issues as the four rivers of Paradise, a favourite
subject in early Christian mosaics in Rome and Ravenna.
Within the garden itself these waters spring up as fountains, springs, and lakes to diversify and refresh the landscape:

> the crisped Brooks,
> Rowling on Orient Pearl and sands of Gold,
> With mazie error under pendant shades
> Ran Nectar, visiting each plant, and fed
> Flours worthy of Paradise which not nice Art
> In Beds and curious Knots, but Nature boon
> Powrd forth profuse on Hill and Dale and Plaine,

Both where the morning Sun first warmly smote
The open field, and where the unpierc't shade
Imbround the noontide Bowrs.[1]

The garden the Lord God planted is not the medieval pleasure-garden of the *Roman de la Rose*, or the old formal garden of Elizabethan and Jacobean times with beds cut out in formal lozenges and squares, trimmed with box-edgings, and with terraces adorned with topiary work. Nor is it one of those wonderful Italian gardens that Milton must have seen on his tour of Italy, an architectural garden. This garden is not something opposed to nature. It is nature idealized and in perfection. It is the new conception of a garden as nature in miniature, where trees, bowers, and fountains, lakes and waterfalls make up a landscape, a conception that comes to perfection in eighteenth-century garden parks and that spread all over Europe as *le jardin anglais*. Milton is of his age in thus picturing the Garden of Eden as a landscape garden, sharing with Marvell's mower a hatred of what 'luxurious man' has made of innocent nature in his gardens.[2] He is all himself in his scorn for 'nice Art' as opposed to 'Nature boon', as in his contempt for

Court Amours
Mixt Dance, or wanton Mask, or Midnight Bal,

as opposed to the exchanges of 'wedded Love'.

We see Paradise first through the eyes of Satan, who comes to destroy it. 'Delicious Paradise' is described as a lovely 'Lantskip'; but its beauty and deliciousness is conveyed to us by appeal to the most immediate of our senses, the physical senses of touch and smell. The purity of the air, the touch of the fresh gales, and the perfumes they carry bring Paradise home to our

[1] *P.L.* IV. 237–46.
[2] 'The Mower against Gardens.'

imaginations as a place of pristine freshness and sweetness:

> As when to them who sail
> Beyond the *Cape of Hope*, and now are past
> *Mozambic*, off at Sea North-East windes blow
> *Sabean* Odours from the spicie shoare
> Of *Arabie* the blest, with such delay
> Well pleas'd they slack thir course, and many a League
> Cheard with the grateful smell old Ocean smiles.
> So entertained those odorous sweets the Fiend
> Who came thir bane.[1]

Milton does not hesitate to tell us that the fruit of Paradise is 'of delicious taste', or to show Adam and Eve lolling on a bank, picking the fruit as it hangs down within easy reach, and chewing the 'savourie pulp'.[2] Paradise is a paradise of all the senses, where the breath of morn is sweet with charm of earliest birds and the earth is fragrant after soft showers.

This Paradise of nature, made by God for man's enjoyment, is left at the close deserted, perhaps to become overgrown tangled thickets, like the wood of the Sleeping Beauty. When the sin of Adam's descendants shall have brought the Flood, it will, as Michael relates, be loosed from its foundations and swept out to sea to become a desolate bare island in the midst of the Southern Ocean:

> Then shall this Mount
> Of Paradise by might of Waves be moovd
> Out of his place, pushd by the horned floud,
> With all his verdure spoil'd, and Trees adrift
> Down the great River to the op'ning Gulf,
> And there take root an Iland salt and bare,
> The haunt of Seales and Orcs, and Sea-mews clang.[3]

No seaman will be lured to slack his course by any grateful smell from this gaunt, salt-encrusted rock. This dis-

---

[1] *P.L.* IV. 159–67. [2] *P.L.* IV. 327–36. [3] *P.L.* XI. 825–31.

lodging of the Mount of Paradise is one of Milton's grand
inventions and it gives him opportunity for a sombre
moral:

> that God attributes to place
> No sanctitie, if none be thither brought.

But, in addition, the uprooting of Paradise allows him,
as he loved to do, to include two different traditions in his
poem. Though by his day it was universally agreed that
Paradise was in Mesopotamia, it had been strongly held
earlier that Paradise was in the Southern Ocean, where
Dante has it, a belief strong enough to have influenced the
direction in which Columbus set sail. Milton, the grand
assimilator, includes both traditions, and makes out of the
conflict of traditions a moving symbol of all that the loss
of Eden means.

Adam and Eve are also first shown to us through
Satan's eyes, as he curiously scans these new creatures.
Milton wants us to see them not as a man and a woman,
but as the first Man and Woman, our great originals, the
pattern after which we are all made. They are not equal

> as their sex not equal seemd;
> For contemplation hee and valour formd,
> For softness shee and sweet attractive Grace,
> Hee for God only, shee for God in him.[1]

No lines have, I suppose, been more quoted and quoted
against Milton than these. But all that is Milton's is the
unequivocal firmness and clarity with which he states the
orthodox view of his age. We find much in Milton's theology repellent because he sets it out so clearly; but there
is little difference, as far as those things that offend us are
concerned, between Milton's system and the system we
could deduce from Donne's sermons or the lyrics of
George Herbert. Similarly, it is a basic assumption of

---

[1] *P.L.* IV. 296–9.

Donne's love poetry that women, as a sex, are inferior to men. He most often, of course, uses this assumption as the basis for hyperbolical compliments to his mistress who is the one great exception, a miracle. Even in those poems in which he treats of a love that is mutual and in which the mistress is the partner in his joy, it is he that is 'all Princes' while she is 'all States'; and in 'Air and Angels' he makes quite clear that man, the active partner, is superior to woman, the passive, that the male is, as Milton says, 'the perfecter sex'.[1] Milton in *Paradise Lost* is not writing a love-poem in which woman is exalted by her lover as the source of all good. He is writing a philosophic epic in which he is embodying his beliefs and the beliefs of his age as to the true nature of things. He is also writing of married love, a theme very rarely touched on by poets, and before Milton very frequently with ribaldry.

The notion that 'masculine' means 'perfect' and 'feminine' means 'imperfect' is a part of a whole way of thinking by which everything was classified and within its class ranged in order: among metals, gold is the best; among trees, the cedar is the noblest; among beasts, the lion is king. If things are not the same, one must be better or perfecter than the other. Masculine meant perfect because man was thought to be complete in himself. Feminine meant imperfect because woman needs man for her perfection. She is not a woman while she is a maid. Eve calls Adam 'My glory, my perfection' because without him her womanhood is incomplete. Donne borrows this notion from its source in Aristotle's *Problems* in the refrain to his 'Epithalamium made at Lincoln's Inn': 'To day put on perfection and a woman's name.' In that enigmatic poem 'The Primrose' he plays with the same idea. Ten, the furthest number since it contains all numbers, is the masculine number; five is the feminine number. Woman needs 'half man', that is five, to become perfect and make

[1] *Apology for Smectymnuus.*

herself up to the perfect number, ten. The notion was based on erroneous conceptions of the nature of the reproductive process: the woman was thought of as contributing nothing but a vessel for the man's seed. It was supported by the Scriptural narrative of Eve's being 'after made, occasional', and, of course, in the seventeenth century the subjection of woman was a theory that corresponded to social and economic facts.

The theory of one sex being the 'perfecter', and indeed the whole conception of the wholly masculine or the wholly feminine in individuals of a species so highly developed biologically as human beings, makes little sense today. It is as outmoded as the equation of sin and guilt is theologically, or as the conflict of Reason and Passion is psychologically. But like all theories that have been seriously held, it has a correspondence with the facts of experience, otherwise men could never have held it. The words, masculine and feminine, are still used by us with their ancient meaning. We say of some women that they have a masculine intellect, and mean it as praise, as we can say in praise of a man that he is as gentle and sensitive as a woman. The general concepts of the ideally masculine and the ideally feminine make sense. Milton is not saying that all men are superior to all women, an idea he flatly denies elsewhere.[1] He is painting an ideal picture in which Adam shows the perfection of physical strength and intellectual power and Eve the perfection of physical grace and moral gentleness. He goes further and does not hesitate to give to Adam the right to 'Absolute rule' and to Eve the duty of 'Subjection'. But this theory of the ideal relation of the sexes does not prevent him from

---

[1] Cf. *Tetrachordon*, where, discussing St. Paul's injunction 'Wives be subject to your husbands', Milton adds: 'Not but that particular exceptions may have place, if she exceed her husband in prudence and dexterity, and he contentedly yield: for then a superior and more natural law comes in, that the wiser should govern the less wise, whether male or female.' I fear one must own that Milton obviously thinks that this situation does not occur very frequently.

presenting with truth and sweetness a relation in which such words as 'Absolute rule' and 'Subjection' seem irrelevant. For Milton most exquisitely sets all the graces of human intercourse in Paradise before the Fall. Adam does not presume on his strength and authority. Made in the image of his Maker, who asks for free love from his creatures, he respects Eve's freedom to grant or deny. Eve, who unlike Satan does not 'disdain subjection', yet wishes to be wooed, to be asked to give what she has no wish to deny; and by 'sweet reluctant amorous delay' she shows that what she has to give is very precious. This courtesy between Adam and Eve, the exchange of roles by which he, the ruler, becomes the suppliant, and she, the ruled, takes the authority he yields to her, is to my mind very beautiful. It is

> Innocence and Virgin Modestie,
> Her vertue and the conscience of her worth,
> That would be woo'd, and not unsought be won,[1]

that makes her turn from Adam when she first sees him. In the exchanges of mutual love there can be no compulsion: 'Love wol nat be constrayned by maystrie.' Love between man and woman is thus an image of the love between God and his creatures, freely given and accepted as a gift.

I cannot share C. S. Lewis's disquiet at Milton's attributing sexual modesty to Eve and allowing her to blush, or his uneasiness at Milton's making it quite clear that there was pleasure in the act of love before the Fall.[2] Eve's blush when Adam leads her 'blushing like the Morn' to their 'Nuptiall Bowre' is not the only blush in the poem. The archangel Raphael, at the mere thought of the loves of the angels, speaks

> with a smile that glow'd
> Celestial rosie red, Loves proper hue.

[1] *P.L.* VIII. 501-3.   [2] *A Preface to 'Paradise Lost'*, pp. 118-20.

Milton will have nothing to do with the horrible patristic conception of the virtuousness of cold copulation. Other feelings than shame make the heart beat faster and bring the blood to the cheeks. But although Milton believes passionately in the goodness of creation and the innocence of natural impulses, he is not a 'simple lifer'. He sees a great gulf fixed between man and the animal creation. The notion of human beings mating as happily and carelessly as birds on the bough is highly un-Miltonic. It is all very well in the Gardens of Adonis for each paramour to know his leman frankly. Spenser's gardens are gardens of myth and his myth is a myth of creation and fecundity. It is different in the historic Garden of Eden where Milton sees the uncorrupted origin of human society and civility. Adam and Eve are creatures of intelligence and moral feeling. He gives Eve therefore modesty, which is not the same as shame, and makes wooing (which is, after all, not unknown among birds and beasts) a part of the Paradisal experience. He shows here the courage of his convictions. To wish him to be more discreet is to wish him to be the less Milton.

He repeatedly uses the word 'mysterious' in this connexion: 'those mysterious parts', 'the Rites mysterious of connubial Love', the 'mysterious reverence' that Adam expresses for 'the genial bed', and the apostrophe 'Haile wedded Love, mysterious Law'. This is not, I think, as C. S. Lewis suggested, an attempt to excuse his 'very unmysterious pictures of Adam and Eve's love-making', and a rather perfunctory one at that; and Lewis's suggestion that he should have 'treated the loves of Adam and Eve as remotely and mysteriously as the loves of the angels' is to use the word 'mysterious' in its modern sense of 'vague' and not as Milton is using it here in its older sense of 'religious', pertaining to what is divinely received and beyond the reach of natural reason. Milton is insisting on the distinction between the human and the animal

creation, in accordance with which the act of generation
in men and women is something more than the act by
which the race is propagated. It is an act by which they
become one flesh, a sacred and sacramental act. What in
the brutes is natural is in man 'mysterious'. Or rather, the
'mysterious' rite of marriage is natural to man. Milton is
writing here in the great Protestant tradition, embodied
in the explanation of the purpose of marriage added to
the Sarum rite in the first Prayer Book of Edward VI[1] and
retained in the marriage service of the Book of Common
Prayer, which held that marriage was 'ordained of God
in the time of man's innocency'. Against the libertine
poets, hymning the 'bel età de l'oro' before social conventions fettered the happy natural freedom of man and
woman to mate and leave their mates as and when they
chose,[2] Milton sets his picture of a golden age in which
the crowning joy is the 'mysterious' union of man and
woman in marriage.

[1] Based on Hermann's *Consultation*, which declares 'how holy a kind of life
and how acceptable to God Matrimony is. For by these places (Gen. ii, Matt.
xix, and Eph. v) we know that God Himself instituted holy wedlock, and that in
paradise, man being yet perfect and holy . . .'.

[2] Cf. such a poem as Donne's 'Confined Love':

> Some man unworthy to be possessor
> Of old or new love, himselfe being false or weake,
>   Thought his paine and shame would be lesser
> If on womankind he might his anger wreake;
>   And thence a law did grow:
>   One should but one man know.
>   But are other creatures so ?
>
> Are Sunne, Moone or Starres by law forbidden
> To smile where they list, or lend away their light ?
>   Are birds divorc'd, or are they chidden
> If they leave their mate, or lie abroad a night ?
>   Beasts doe no joyntures lose
>   Though they new lovers choose,
>   But we are made worse then those.

The main sources of this fashionable naturalism are the speech of Myrrha in
Ovid's *Metamorphoses* (x. 320 et seq.) and the chorus from Tasso's *Aminta*, 'O
bel età de l'oro'.

Here again, as with Paradise itself, we are shown a contrast; love before and love after the Fall. The flowery setting is the same, the age-old setting, as Professor Bush pointed out,[1] for the loves of the Gods, and also for the loves of nymphs and shepherds. But after the Fall there is no wooing and, of course, no prayer. Adam instead 'forbore not glance or toy of amorous intent', and Eve's eye 'darted contagious Fire':

> Her hand he seis'd, and to a shadie bank,
> Thick overhead with verdant roof imbowr'd
> He led her nothing loath.[2]

Before the Fall it is the pleasure of touch that Milton insists on. After the Fall it is the roving lascivious eye, the nobler intellectual sense of sight, that reigns and incites to lust. The enjoyment of touch and taste and smell, the purely sensuous senses, is the mark of Paradise and the state of innocence. To adapt a line of Donne, Milton first shows us a love that is 'peace', in which 'sweet reluctant amorous delay' plays its part, and then a love that is 'rage', a greedy coupling.

The doctrine of woman's natural inferiority to man is insisted on more than once in the poem. But it might well be argued that in his actual presentation of Adam and Eve Milton gives Eve the advantage in moral and spiritual qualities. It is Adam who begins their bitter quarrel and is the first to say 'It was all your fault'. And nothing could exceed in dignity Eve's simple Scriptural reply to her Judge; it makes Adam's sound loquacious and self-conscious:

> To whom sad *Eve* with shame nigh overwhelm'd,
> Confessing soon, yet not before her Judge
> Bold or loquacious, thus abasht repli'd.
>   The Serpent me beguil'd and I did eate.[3]

---

[1] 'Paradise Lost' in Our Time, Cornell University Press, 1945, pp. 105-6.
[2] P.L. IX. 1037-9.   [3] P.L. X. 159-62.

One thinks of all the satire on feminine garrulity that these lines quietly reject. It is Eve who seeks Adam out where he lies lamenting on the ground and is not repulsed by his bitterly cruel speech. If she led Adam to sin, she also leads him to penitence. Her penitence and grief awaken his love and pity, and her impulsive generosity in wishing to take all the punishment brings him to a true sense of their common plight. As she seeks him in tears and penitence for having sinned against him, she shows him the way by which they may both find pardon; and when Adam feels the persuasion that his prayer is heard he turns to Eve and greets her solemnly with a new name. So far she has been

> Sole partner and sole part of all these joyes . . .;
>
> Daughter of God and Man, accomplisht Eve . . .;
>
> Blest Image of myself and dearer half . . .;
>
> Sole Eve, Associate sole, to me beyond
> Compare above all living Creatures deare . . .;
>
> O fairest of Creation, last and best . . .;[1]

now he adopts the greeting Raphael had addressed to her, and hails her with the same solemn and prophetic *Ave*:

> Whence Haile to thee
> *Eve* rightly call'd, Mother of all Mankind,
> Mother of all things living, since by thee
> Man is to live, and all things live for Man.[2]

It is as mother and cherisher that Milton presents her lamenting her expulsion from Paradise:

> O flours
> That never will in other Climate grow,
> My early visitation, and my last
> At Eev'n, which I bred up with tender hand
> From the first op'ning bud, and gave ye Names,

[1] *P.L.* IV. 411; IV. 660; V. 95; IX. 227–8; IX. 896.
[2] *P.L.* XI. 158–61.

Who now shall reare ye to the Sun, or ranke
Your Tribes, and water from th'ambrosial Fount?
Thee lastly nuptial Bowre, by mee adornd
With what to sight or smell was sweet; from thee
How shall I part, and whither wander down
Into a lower World, to this obscure
And wilde, how shall we breath in other Aire
Less pure, accustomd to immortal Fruits?[1]

Every woman going into exile is speaking. To Adam,
Paradise is the place where he spoke with God. To Eve,
it is the garden she had worked in, the plants she had
reared, the Bower her hands had made: her home. Eve
sleeps while the angel shows Adam visions of things to
come; but while she sleeps she is visited by gentle dreams,
and it is to her that Milton gives the last word. Unselfish
love and humility, the most attractive of all virtues, are
here given consummate expression:

Whence thou returnst, & whither wentst, I know;
For God is also in sleep, and Dreams advise,
Which he hath sent propitious, some great good
Presaging, since with sorrow and hearts distress
Wearied I fell asleep: but now lead on;
In mee is no delay; with thee to goe,
Is to stay here; without thee here to stay,
Is to go hence unwilling; thou to mee
Art all things under Heav'n, all places thou,
Who for my wilful crime art banisht hence.
This further consolation yet secure
I carry hence; though all by mee is lost,
Such favour I unworthie am voutsaft,
By mee the Promis'd Seed shall all restore.[2]

Eve's cry 'Without thee here to stay is to go hence
unwilling' echoes two earlier affirmations of passionate
love in the poem. Unfallen, in what is, perhaps, the most

---

[1] *P.L.* XI. 273-85.   [2] *P.L.* XII. 610-23.

beautiful lyrical passage in *Paradise Lost*, Eve turns her praise of the beauties of Paradise to the praise of love:

> But neither breath of Morn when she ascends
> With charm of earliest Birds, nor rising Sun
> On this delightful land, nor herb, fruit, floure,
> Glistring with dew, nor fragrance after showers,
> Nor grateful Evening mild, nor silent Night
> With this her solemn Bird, nor walk by Moon,
> Or glittering Starr-light without thee is sweet.[1]

And at the crisis of the action, in perhaps the most poignant moment of the poem, Adam sees all the sensuous beauty of Paradise fade into desolation at the thought of being in Paradise alone, without Eve:

> How can I live without thee, how forgoe
> Thy sweet Converse and Love so dearly joyn'd,
> To live again in these wilde Woods forlorn?[2]

Milton surely intended us to hear these echoes. Eve sinned by being 'bold and adventurous', qualities Milton, with his age, thought inappropriate in a woman. Adam sinned by being dependent on another, a quality inappropriate in a man. What Eve, whether sinless or penitent, rightly says, Adam says wrongly. Adam cannot endure the thought of life without Eve. It is a sophistication to say that he dies *for* her; he decides to die *with* her. His motive is not the desire to share her punishment, to make it lighter. The truth rings out in his cry: he cannot live without her. It is for his own sake, to escape the horror of solitude, for the sake of love, rather than for her sake, that he decides to share her fate, whatever it may be. In Milton's view this is effeminacy.

Professor Waldock thought that the whole poem collapsed at this point because every right human instinct and all our moral feelings are with Adam and must applaud

---

[1] *P.L.* IV. 650-6.   [2] *P.L.* IX. 908-10.

his resolution to die with Eve rather than to live innocent and sinless without her. The problem on the human level is essentially the same, if there is any problem in either case, as the problem that the heroic virtues of Satan present on the cosmic level. As Milton did not have to prove that Satan was wicked and could therefore allow him many splendid archangelic virtues, so he did not have to prove that the eating of the apple was a disastrous act, harmless and insignificant in itself, appalling and significant in what it implied and in its consequences, like, 'to compare great things with small', Caesar's crossing of the Rubicon. The Rubicon is a feeble little stream, if the trickle to which Mussolini gave the title is indeed the Rubicon. A child could wade across it. The crossing of it was a decisive and irreversible act. The apple is, in itself, nothing. It is everything because God's command has made it so. For seventeen centuries the trivial act of eating the forbidden fruit had gathered to itself a weight of religious feeling and awe. It was the sign and token of man's refusal to fulfil the prime end of his creation: to glorify God and enjoy him forever. The act was so universally significant that, as I have said, Milton could present it with no elaboration and no attempt to arouse in us any sense of horror. It is enough for him to say 'she pluck'd, she eat', and 'he scrupl'd not to eat'. Relying here on a universal response, Milton could allow to Eve and to Adam nobility of motive, or, as in all tragic acts, a mixture of the noble and the base. Having insisted that the mutual love of man and woman is the highest earthly good, that to be 'imparadis'd in one another's arms' is the 'happier Eden', and that in our fallen world the source of 'Relations dear and all the Charities' is to be found in wedded love, Milton gives to Adam a motive it is impossible not to sympathize with, and that sets in the clearest possible light the meaning of the ancient story. When the Jews took over the Babylonian story of the Garden and the Tree of Life that stood in the midst of it, their religious genius infused into the story a meaning that it lacked before. It seems to have been originally a story to explain death, a fact that primitive thought seems always to feel to need explanation. Man lost his immortality because the agile serpent raced him to the Tree of Life and deprived him of a boon meant for him. The Jews added the second tree, the Tree of the Knowledge of Good and Evil, or of happiness and misery, the tree of experience, and made death the consequence of man's violation of the command of his Maker, linking death with sin. The story as thus reshaped expressed the profound conviction of the Jews that sin is primarily an offence against God, not a social offence, and that it is a wilful offence. The 'mysterious' prohibition, and I use the word in its ancient sense, meaning that it is beyond reasonable explanation, is a religious prohibition. This is why Satan cannot understand it and thinks the whole affair ludicrous:

> Him by fraud I have seduc'd
> From his Creator, and the more to increase
> Your wonder, with an Apple; he thereat
> Offended, worth your laughter, hath giv'n up
> Both his beloved Man and all his World
> To Sin and Death a prey.[1]

The medieval carol makes the same point, though to a different end: 'And all was for an appel, an appel taken was.' The uneaten apple is the pledge and sign of man's obedience to God, the token that all is His. It corresponds to such features of Jewish religion as the strict dietary laws, the first fruits, the tenth dedicated to God as token for all, the strict Sabbath rest. These are all visible and perpetual signs of man's recognition of God's supreme claim, above all other claims: that all we use and enjoy is ultimately His. The command that is transgressed must

[1] *P.L.* x. 485–90.

be an irrational one in order that it may be purely religious.
Eve understands this perfectly well. This command is 'sole
Daughter of his voice';

> the rest, we live
> Law to our selves, our Reason is our Law.[1]

All other actions they may weigh and consider, choosing
by the light of reason between what is right and wrong.
This one act cannot be argued over. There are no reasons
for or against eating the fruit, the act is in itself morally
neutral. Satan's skill lies in suggesting to Eve that the
matter can be argued over, that there are reasons why
she should eat which are better than the reasons why she
should not. Adam is not thus deceived, though he finds
sophisticated arguments, once his mind is made up, to
suggest that the offence is less grave or that punishment
may not follow. He knows that the act is sin. He eats
because he cannot bear to be parted from Eve. 'The Bond
of Nature' draws him:

> Our State cannot be severd, we are one,
> One Flesh; to loose thee were to loose my self.[2]

Milton thus places in stark opposition the Bond of
Nature and the claim of God, remembering, no doubt,
such texts as the severe Lucan saying: 'If any man cometh
unto me and hateth not his own father and mother and
wife and children and brethren and sisters, yea and his
own life also, he cannot be my disciple.' A sharp contrast to Adam clinging to Eve is given us by Milton's
greatest contemporary, Bunyan, in his picture of Christian
at the opening of *The Pilgrim's Progress*:

So I saw in my Dream, that the Man began to run; Now he had
not run far from his own door, but his Wife and Children perceiving
it began to cry after him to return: but the Man put his fingers in
his Ears, and ran on crying, Life, Life, Eternal Life: so he looked
not before him but fled towards the middle of the Plain.

[1] *P.L.* IX. 653-4.   [2] *P.L.* IX. 958-9.

Bunyan set in the margin the reference Luke xiv. 26, the text that I have just quoted.

Donne, who is so often contrasted with Milton, to Milton's disadvantage, as a poet of human love, is no less severe than Milton in his recognition that the 'Bond of Nature' belongs to the natural man and that in the Kingdom of Heaven there is neither marrying nor giving in marriage, nor husband, wife, father, or son. His sonnet on his own beloved wife's death ascribes his loss to God's 'tender jealousy' that fears lest he allow his love 'to saints and angels, things divine', and in a letter to his mother to comfort her on her daughter's death he writes in the same strain:

> God hath seemed to repent, that he allowed any part of your life any earthly happinesse, that he might keep your Soul in continuall exercise, and longing, and assurance, of comming immediately to him. . . . His purpose is, to remove out of your heart, all such love of this world's happinesse, as might put Him out of possession of it. He will have you entirelie.[1]

Accepting, and expecting us to accept, that obedience to God is an absolute, Milton, in consonance with his whole treatment of his subject, makes Adam fall away from his Creator for the highest human good, and spurn the Giver for the most precious of all his temporal gifts.

After the climax of the action there is naturally a fall in tension. The last two books present to us, in visions which summarize the world's history, the world we all know, the world of sickness, toil, and death, of wars, tyrannies, and disasters. Adam has to take all this into his consciousness, and accommodate his imagination to the weight of human sin and human misery. These visions of the world's woes belong to Milton's first conception of his poem. They were to be presented as allegorical pageants in the tragedies he drafted in 1641. It is false, I think, to suggest

---

[1] *A Collection of Letters made by Sir Tobie Mathews*, 1660, pp. 325-7.

that the last two books are the work of an older and dis-
illusioned man who had lost the vigour and ardour with
which he set out on his epic and who was discouraged by
the failure of his political hopes.[1] It is naïve to think of a
poem such as *Paradise Lost* being written sequentially,
and of Milton beginning at the beginning and going on
steadily to the end. And at whatever time these books
were composed, a tone of sadness at the close was inseparable from the subject that Milton chose. A poem
whose title is *Paradise Lost* must of necessity end sorrow-
fully. The buoyancy and imaginative vigour of the first
books breaks out again in Book X in Satan's meeting with
Sin and Death, in the dramatic return of Satan to the
Metropolis of Hell, when he passes

> through the midst unmarkt,
> In shew plebeian Angel militant
> Of lowest order,[2]

takes his seat invisible, and then bursts out in 'sudden
blaze' with his exultant speech of triumph, and in the
final extraordinary and daring fantasy of the metamor-
phosis of Satan and his angels into serpents swarming up
the trees of the Grove of Hell to eat their Dead-sea fruit.
Energy of imagination and freedom of invention belong
to the cosmic theme. Here the triumph of good is assured
and the imagination is unfettered by the sad actualities of
experience. The human and historic theme demands a
different handling. The tone of sorrow consoled by hope
with which the poem ends is the only tolerable tone for
the close. On the cosmic level the grand scheme of Providence bringing good out of evil, shapes the whole design:
it is presented to Adam as doctrine by Michael. On the
human level Milton can only celebrate the secret victory
of the 'upright heart and pure', and for the loveliness of

[1] Professor F. T. Prince's essay 'On the last two books of *Paradise Lost*'
(*Essays and Studies*, 1958) is a masterly defence of the structural necessity and
poetical merits of the closing books. [2] *P.L.* x. 441–3.

the Paradise that is lost offer us the 'Paradise within', which cannot be rendered to the imagination in sensuous terms. He brings us at the close to life as we know it, where the triumph of good is matter for faith and future hope, not matter of experience. When Milton abandoned the idea of writing a patriotic epic, and decided not to sing the triumphs of his own land or the prowess of some Christian hero or champion but to take for his hero the prototype of all mankind, he committed himself to a poem that must end inconclusively. It is not possible, if one looks at the history of the human race and attempts to write a poem that shall illuminate the human condition here and now, to end with anything else but a 'conclusion in which nothing is concluded'. To the religious mind the story is not complete and never can be complete in this world. To the agnostic it is equally true that the story of mankind is a story without an end. Fifty years ago it might have been plausible to complain, as some critics did, that Milton's pageant of human ills and his picture of human history was too gloomy and gave too little credit to the achievements of the human race and to man's progress in civility. The complaint seems less plausible today. Murder, luxury, war, luxury, disaster, the corruptions of selfishness in peace, the devastations of war, tyrannies, cruel oppressions, enslavements of whole peoples—the pattern that Milton creates out of the early chapters of Genesis seems a familiar enough historic pattern, and we may all echo Adam's lament as he sees fierce warriors swooping down on a peaceful pastoral people in the first battle:

> O what are these,
> Deaths Ministers, not Men, who thus deal Death
> Inhumanly to men, and multiply
> Ten thousand fould the sin of him who slew
> His Brother; for of whom such massacher
> Make they but of thir Brethren, men of men?[1]

[1] *P.L.* XI. 671–6.

Paradise Lost could never have ended any way but sadly, at whatever time of his life Milton had written it. But we cannot doubt that his long delay in writing his master-work was to our infinite gain. His experience of great political events gives the poem much of its dramatic reality, and the disappointment of his hopes, personal and political, gives it depth. A weight of human experience and knowledge of men and a weight of human suffering is in the poem which the Milton of the 1640's could not have brought to it. So that when he finally carried his poem to completion he produced a work that contains both the imaginative vigour, inventiveness, richness of detail, and strength of design that are characteristic of the works of an artist's maturity and the spiritual qualities that move us so deeply in late works, where the meaning the artist is striving to express is so important to him that it overwhelms his delight in the means of expression. Milton had had to learn patience in a hard school, the most difficult of all the virtues to one of his enthusiastic and passionate temperament. Too much has been made of Milton's asperities. We may well believe that 'he pronounced the letter R. very hard—a certaine signe of a satyricall witt'.[1] There is a good deal of satirical wit and of the sardonic in *Paradise Lost*. It adds a salt and savour without which the poem would be poorer; but it is a minor element in the whole. The impression with which we end is a mingled one: of awe at the 'vast Design' and admiration for the courage that set out upon and carried through so profoundly original an enterprise, and for the wealth of knowledge Milton brought to adorn his great argument; but also of reverence for the final simplicity of what *Paradise Lost* has to say of our human condition. Milton leaves us at the close with his own hard-won knowledge that patience, 'the bearing well of all calamities', faith, and peace of

---

[1] Aubrey, *Brief Lives*, edited by Clark, 1898, ii. 67.

conscience are the only weapons that can never fail in 'the wilderness of this world':

> Henceforth I learne, that to obey is best,
> And love with feare the onely God, to walk
> As in his presence, ever to observe
> His providence, and on him sole depend,
> Merciful over all his works, with good
> Still overcoming evil, and by small
> Accomplishing great things, by things deemd weak
> Subverting worldly strong, and worldly wise
> By simply meek; that suffering for Truths sake
> Is fortitude to highest victorie,
> And to the faithful Death the Gate of Life.[1]

I quoted Coleridge on Satan. I end with quoting Coleridge on the experience of reading and re-reading *Paradise Lost*:

No one can rise from the perusal of this immortal poem without a deep sense of the grandeur and purity of Milton's soul. . . . He was, as every great poet has ever been, a good man; but finding it impossible to realize his own aspirations, either in religion, or politics, or society, he gave up his heart to the living spirit and light within him, and avenged himself on the world by enriching it with this record of his own transcendent ideal.[2]

---

[1] *P.L.* XII. 560–71.
[2] *Miscellaneous Criticism*, edited by Raysor, 1936, p. 165.

APPENDIX A

Milton's Satan and the Theme of Damnation in Elizabethan Tragedy[1]

WE are all familiar with the progeny of Milton's Satan and the effort of most recent criticism has been directed towards clearing the Satan of Milton's poem from his associations with the Promethean rebel of romantic tradition. But the question whether Satan had any ancestors has hardly been raised, or has been dismissed by reference to the devil of popular tradition, or by an allusion to the heroic figure of the Old English *Genesis B*. The late Mr. Charles Williams, in an essay on Milton which seems likely to become a classic, and Mr. C. S. Lewis, building, as he delighted to own, on Mr. Williams, destroyed, one hopes for ever, the notion that Satan had grounds for his rebellion.[2] But when we have agreed that Satan's 'wrongs' which 'exceed all measure' exist only in Shelley's generous imagination, and that it is easier to draw a bad character than a good, and have assented to the statement that Satan's career is a steady progress from bad to worse and ends with his complete deformity, we still have no explanations of why the Romantic critics stood *Paradise Lost* on its head, or why the 'common reader' finds the imaginative impact of the first books so much more powerful than that of the last, or why, as one re-reads the poem, the exposure of Satan's malice and meanness seems curiously irrelevant. There remains always, untouched by the argument, the image of enormous pain and eternal loss. It is out of key with the close of the poem, which does not drive it from our memory, or absorb it.

'From hero to general, from general to politician, from politician to secret service agent, and thence to a thing that peers in at bedroom or bathroom windows, and thence to a toad, and finally to a snake—such is the progress of Satan', writes Mr. Lewis, and he

[1] Reprinted from *English Studies 1948*, being volume one of the new series of *Essays and Studies*, 1948.

[2] See *The English Poems of Milton*, with a preface by Charles Williams (World's Classics), 1940, and C. S. Lewis, *A Preface to Paradise Lost*, 1942.

rightly declares that there is no question of Milton's beginning by making Satan too glorious and then, too late, attempting to rectify the error. 'Such an unerring picture of "the sense of injured merit" in its actual operations upon character cannot have come about by blundering and accident.' We can parallel this account of the career of Satan, but not from Iago and Becky Sharp, whom Mr. Lewis cites as examples of bad characters who are more interesting than their virtuous opposites. From a brave and loyal general, to a treacherous murderer, to a hirer of assassins, to an employer of spies, to a butcher, to a coward, to a thing with no feeling for anything but itself, to a monster and a 'hell-hound': that is a summary of the career of Macbeth. From a proud philosopher, master of all human knowledge, to a trickster, to a slave of phantoms, to a cowering wretch: that is a brief sketch of the progress of Dr. Faustus. With varying use of mythological machinery, this theme of the deforming of a creature in its origin bright and good, by its own willed persistence in acts against its own nature, is handled by Shakespeare and Marlowe, and with great power, but in a purely naturalistic setting, by Middleton and Rowley in *The Changeling*. It is on the tragic stage that we find the idea of damnation in English literature before *Paradise Lost*. 'Satan', writes Mr. Williams, 'is the Image of personal clamour for personal independence.' He is in rebellion against 'the essential fact of things'. The same can be said of Faustus, of Macbeth, and of Beatrice-Joanna, and it is particularly interesting to notice that in *Macbeth* and *The Changeling* the dramatists have altered their sources to bring out the full implications of the theme.

The devil was a comic character in the medieval drama; in the Elizabethan period he virtually disappears in his own person from the greater plays. But what Mr. Lewis calls 'the Satanic predicament' is there, and it appears in the tragic, not the comic, mode of vision. The terrible distinction between devils and men in popular theology lay in the irreversibility of the fall of the angels. Unlike men the fallen angels were incapable of repentance and so for them there was no pardon. As Donne puts it: 'To those that fell, can appertaine no reconciliation; no more then to those that die in their sins; for *Quod homini mors, Angelis casus*; The fall of the Angels wrought upon them, as the death of a man does upon him; They are both equally incapable of change to better.'[1] Donne recognizes that

[1] *LXXX Sermons*, 1640, p. 9. A recent reading of Donne's *Sermons* for another

some of the Fathers thought that 'the devil retaining still his faculty of free will, is therefore capable of repentance, and so of benefit by this coming of Christ';[1] but this is exactly the point which Aquinas denies and Donne assents to his view. Aquinas decides that the fallen angels cannot repent, since, though they know the beginnings of penitence in fear, their free will is perverted: 'Quidquid in eis est naturale, totum est bonum et ad bonum inclinans, sed liberum arbitrium in eis est in malo obstinatum; et quia motus virtutis et vitii non sequitur inclinationem naturae, sed magis motum liberi arbitrii; ideo non oportet, quamvis naturaliter inclinentur ad bonum, quod motus virtutis in eis sit, vel esse possit.'[2] In the tragic world of Faustus and Macbeth we find presented to us in human terms this incapacity for change to a better state. It never occurs to us that Macbeth will turn back, or indeed that he can; and though Marlowe, in this more merciful, as he is always more metaphysical, than Shakespeare, keeps before us the fact of Faustus's humanity by the urgings of the Good Angel, yet to the Good Angel's 'Faustus, repent; yet God will pity thee', comes at once the Bad Angel's response: 'Thou art a spirit;[3] God cannot pity thee'; and to Faustus's

> Who buzzeth in mine ears, I am a spirit?
> Be I a devil, yet God may pity me;
> Yea, God will pity me, if I repent.

comes the confident statement of the Bad Angel: 'Ay, but Faustus never shall repent'; to which Faustus gives a despairing assent: 'My heart is harden'd, I cannot repent.'[4]

purpose has impressed upon me how often Donne provides the comment of a theologian or a moralist upon the tragedies of his contemporaries.

[1] Ibid., p. 66.   [2] S.T., Supplement, Q. XVI, Art. 3.

[3] Spirit here as elsewhere in the play means evil spirit, or devil.

[4] All quotations from Dr. Faustus are from the edition of Dr. F. S. Boas, 1932. The point that Faustus is presented to us as incapable of real repentance, though like the devils he knows the beginnings of penitence in fear and 'believes and trembles', is obscured if we accept, as Dr. Boas does, the suggestion of Mr. H. T. Baker (Modern Language Notes, vol. xxi, pp. 86–87) and transfer to Faustus the close of the Old Man's speech in Act V, scene 1 (p. 161). In this most touching scene the Old Man makes a last appeal to Faustus to remember his humanity:

> Though thou hast now offended like a man,
> Do not persever in it like a devil;
> Yet, yet, thou hast an amiable soul,
> If sin by custom grow not into nature.

H

In the three plays mentioned, along with this incapacity for change to a better state, or repentance, go two other closely related ideas. The initial act is an act against nature, it is a primal sin, in that it contradicts the 'essential fact of things', and its author knows that it does so. It is not an act committed by mistake; it is not an error of judgement, it is an error of will. The act is unnatural and so are its results; it deforms the nature which performs it. The second idea is the irony of retributive justice. The act is performed for an imagined good, which appears so infinitely desirable that the conditions for its supposed satisfaction are accepted; but a rigorous necessity reigns and sees to it that though the conditions are exacted literally, the desire is only granted ironically, and this is inevitable, since the desire is for something forbidden by the very nature of man.[1]

We are unfortunate in possessing Marlowe's greatest play only in an obviously mutilated form; but in spite of possible distortion and some interpolation in the centre, the grandeur of the complete reversal stands out clearly. Apart from its opening and concluding choruses, which provide an archaic framework, and the short closing scene in the 1616 text, where the scholars find the mangled body of Faustus, the play begins and ends with the hero in his study. In the first scene Faustus runs through all the branches of human knowledge and finds them inadequate to his desires. Logic can only teach argument; medicine stops short where human desire is most thwarted, since it cannot defeat death; law is a mercenary pursuit; and divinity, which he comes to last, holds the greatest disappointment: it is grounded in the recognition of man's mortality and his fallibility. The two texts from Jerome's Bible insult his aspiration: *Stipendium peccati mors est*, and *Si peccasse negamus, fallimur, et nulla est in nobis veritas*.[2] He turns instead to magic because it is:

---

[1] Donne supplies us with a comment on the 'omnipotence' of Faustus, the 'kingship' of Macbeth, and the 'marriage' of Beatrice-Joanna, when he says: 'For small wages, and ill-paid pensions we serve him (Satan); and lest any man should flatter and delude himselfe, in saying, I have my wages, and my reward before hand, my pleasures in this life, the punishment, (if ever) not till the next, The Apostle destroyes that dreame, with that question of confusion, *What fruit had you then in those things, of which you are now ashamed?* Certainly sin is not a gainfull way; . . . fruitlessness, unprofitableness before, shame and dishonor after.' *LXXX Sermons*, p. 65.

[2] It is worth noting that Faustus does not complete the text, which is familiar from its use as one of the Sentences. 'If we say that we have no sin, we deceive

a world of profit and delight,
Of power, of honour, and omnipotence.

He decides to 'tire his brains to get a deity'. The sin of Faustus here
is presumption, the aspiring above his order, or the rebellion against
the law of his creation.

But when he is last seen alone in his study it is the opposite sin
which delivers him to damnation: the final sin of Faustus is despair.[1]
However much he may call in his fear on God or Christ, it is the
power of Lucifer and the bond with Lucifer which he really believes
in. It is to Lucifer he prays: 'O, spare me, Lucifer!' and 'Ah, rend
not my heart for naming of my Christ!' Donne gives presumption
and despair as one of the couples which the Schoolmen have called
sins against the Holy Ghost 'because naturally they shut out those
meanes by which the Holy Ghost might work upon us . . . for presumption takes away the feare of God, and desperation the love of

ourselves, and the truth is not in us: but, if we confess our sins, he is faithful and
just to forgive us our sins, and to cleanse us from all unrighteousness.'
    [1] The word *despair* or its derivative *desperate* occurs thirteen times in the play.
See I. 3. 91; II. 1. 4 and 5; II. 2. 25 and 31; IV. 5a. 31; V. 1. 64, 68, 72, and 79;
V. 2. 11, 92, and 101.
    In *The Conflict of Conscience* by Nathaniell Woodes, Minister of Norwich,
published 1581 (Hazlitt-Dodsley, vol. vi), in which we can see the old morality
play of wrongful choice, punishment, repentance, and forgiveness turning into
the Elizabethan tragedy of sin and retribution, the whole struggle in the final
act is between the hero's despair and the efforts of his friends to convince him
that he is not beyond God's mercy. One can commend the enterprise if not the
success of the Minister of Norwich in trying to put the finer points of the doctrine
of justification by faith into fourteeners. Poor as his play is, it shows in a most
interesting way the great debate of the sixteenth and seventeenth centuries on the
freedom of the will being turned into drama. In *The Conflict of Conscience*, at the
very last moment, faith conquers, and the happy ending of the old morality is
preserved. [When I wrote this I was unaware that the play is found in two issues.
As originally published it ended, as in life, with the hero (Francis Spira) commit-
ting suicide. In the second issue his name was removed from the title-page and a
happy ending was substituted. See the Malone Society reprint.] In *Dr. Faustus*,
which retains formally much of the old morality, despair triumphs. Our understanding of some of the tragedies of Shakespeare and his contemporaries might
be enriched if we thought more in terms of

Providence, Foreknowledge, Will, and Fate,
Fixt Fate, free will, foreknowledge absolute,

and less in terms of 'fatal flaws' and 'errors of judgement'.

God'.¹ They are the two faces of the sin of Pride. Faustus tormen-
ted by devils is obsessed by their power; but the Old Man is safe from
them, because of his faith. The great reversal from the first scene
of Dr. Faustus to the last can be defined in different ways: from
presumption to despair; from doubt of the existence of hell to belief
in the reality of nothing else; from a desire to be more than man to
the recognition that he has excluded himself from the promise of
redemption for all mankind in Christ; from haste to sign the bond
to desire for delay when the moment comes to honour it; from
aspiration to deity and omnipotence to longing for extinction. At
the beginning Faustus wished to rise above his humanity; at the
close he would sink below it, be transformed into a beast or into
'little water drops'. At the beginning he attempts usurpation upon
God; at the close he is an usurper upon the Devil.²

As for the reward Faustus obtains, it is difficult to argue from the
play as it has come down to us, and one should not in fairness say
that Faustus appears to sell his soul for the satisfaction of playing
practical jokes. But there are two episodes of some significance near
the beginning, in which Marlowe's hand is clearly apparent, which
it is possible to argue from. Faustus takes Mephistophilis as his
servant; he demands twenty-four years of 'all voluptuousness'

> Having thee ever to attend on me,
> To give me whatsoever I shall ask,
> To tell me whatsoever I demand,
>
> .   .   .   .   .   .
>
> And always be obedient to my will.

As the play proceeds it is clear what happens with the last clause
of the agreement: the obedient servant becomes the master. It is

¹ *LXXX Sermons*, p. 349.

² 'The greatest sin that ever was, and that upon which even the blood of
Christ Jesus hath not wrought, the sin of Angels was that *Similis ero Altissimo*, to
be like God. To love our selves, to be satisfied in our selves, to finde an omni-
sufficiency in our selves, is an intrusion, an usurpation upon God.' Ibid., p. 156.
'Did God ordain hell fire for us? no, but for the Devil and his Angels. And yet
we that are vessels so broken, as that there is not a sheard left, to fetch water at
the pit, that is, no means in our selves, to derive one drop of Christ's blood upon
us, nor to wring out one tear of true repentance from us, have plung'd our selves
into this everlasting, and this dark fire, which was not prepared for us: A wretched
covetousness, to be intruders upon the Devil; a wretched ambition, to be usur-
pers upon damnation.' *XXVI Sermons*, 1660, p. 273.

Mephistophilis who speaks with authority as representative of 'great Lucifer', and it is Faustus who obeys. But it is the same with the other two clauses. Immediately after the bond is signed Faustus begins to ask questions, and he asks about hell. He receives what are in the context of the play true answers, but he does not believe them. He thinks hell a fable, and Mephistophilis with melancholy irony leaves the subject: 'Ay, think so, till experience change thy mind.' Then Faustus makes his first request: he asks for a wife. Here the text is plainly defective; the verse breaks down into half-lines and prose, a devil enters dressed as a woman with fireworks attached which explode. But after this horseplay, Mephistophilis resumes in dignified Marlovian verse:

> Marriage is but a ceremonial toy:
> And if thou lovest me, think no more of it.
> I'll cull thee out the fairest courtesans,
> And bring them ev'ry morning to thy bed:
> She whom thine eye shall like, thy heart shall have.

If we turn to the source, the English Faust Book, we can, I think, see the implications of the scene and conjecture why Marlowe set it here.

Doctor *Faustus* . . . bethinking himselfe of a wife called Mephistophiles to counsaile; which would in no wise agree: demanding of him if he would breake the couenant made with him or if hee had forgot it. Hast thou not (quoth *Mephistophiles*) sworne thy selfe an enemy to God and all creatures? To this I answere thee, thou canst not marry; thou canst not serue two masters, God, and my Prince: for wedlock is a chiefe institution ordained of God, and that hast thou promised to defie, as we doe all, and that hast thou also done: and moreouer thou hast confirmed it with thy blood: perswade thy selfe, that what thou doost in contempt of wedlock, it is all to thine own delight.

When Faustus persists in his demand, an ugly devil appears and offers himself as a bride. On his vanishing Mephistophilis reappears to say: 'It is no iesting with us, holde thou that which thou hast vowed, and wee will perform as wee haue promised.'[1] The point of the scene is clear even in the play as we have it: Faustus's first request is met with a refusal. The source gives the full implications of that refusal, which may have been cut out to allow for more

---

[1] *Dr. Faustus*, ed. cit., Appendix I, pp. 181–2.

fireworks: marriage and 'the finest courtesans' are incompatibles. Faustus has not exchanged limitations for freedom; he has merely exchanged one kind of limitation for another. Marriage belongs to the world he has left. He cannot have all he wants, for the satisfaction of some desires involves the thwarting of others.

It is the same with knowledge soon after. Faustus disputes with Mephistophilis of 'divine astrology'. The answers he gets he dismisses with contempt; he knew them already. But then he goes on to ask the great question:

Faust. Well, I am answer'd. Now tell me who made the world.
Meph. I will not.
Faust. Sweet Mephistophilis, tell me.
Meph. Move me not, Faustus.
Faust. Villain, have I not bound thee to tell me any thing?
Meph. Ay, that is not against our kingdom.
　　　That is: thou art damn'd; think thou of hell.

Some kinds of knowledge, like some kinds of experience, Faustus has shut himself off from. He has not escaped the necessity of choice. It is a chosen path he follows to the end. Marlowe does all he can by the device of the two angels to keep before us that Faustus is still a man, and that repentance is open to him, if he will only

　　　　　Call for mercy, and avoid despair.

But he persists. His rewards are the delights of the imagination, sweet and terrible fantasies, culminating in the vision of Helen,[1] and the exercise of what power Mephistophilis allows him, for the practical jokes probably represent a debasing rather than an alteration of Marlowe's intention. But knowledge and felicity he has exchanged for shadows, and for power he gets slavery.

The theme of damnation was explicit for Marlowe in the story he dramatized. Shakespeare reads it into the story of Macbeth, or rather he shapes his material to bring out the same fundamental conceptions as are embodied in the Faustus myth. The story is

---

[1] Dr. Greg has recently recovered for us the full mingling of horror and beauty in the scene in which Faustus embracing Helen cries: 'Her lips suck forth my soul: see where it flies!' He points out that Helen is a 'spirit' and that in this play a spirit is a devil. 'Faustus commits the sin of demoniality, that is bodily intercourse with demons.' See W. W. Greg, 'The Damnation of Faustus', *Modern Language Review*, April 1946, pp. 97–107.

fully developed in terms of human beings and their relations to each other. Macbeth's crime is a crime against his fellow men, against society, and this provides Shakespeare with what Marlowe found so difficult to construct, a proper middle to his play. But even so *Macbeth* is by far the shortest of the great tragedies, in spite of having far the longest exposition, and, as Bradley noted, its minor characters are singularly lifeless and uninteresting. The interest is concentrated almost wholly on Macbeth and his wife.

The crime that Macbeth commits is, as has been pointed out, without any of the excuses which the source offered. A quite different play could have been made out of Holinshed's narrative; Shakespeare might have written the tragedy of a brave and able man, impatient at misgovernment, killing a weak and ineffective king, and being corrupted by the evil means he had chosen to a supposedly good end. There is a rational motive too in another story from which Shakespeare took the details of the murder, for Donwald, who slew King Duff, was avenging his kinsfolk, who had been barbarously punished by the king. But Shakespeare's Duncan is blameless and kingly, and he has paid all honour to Macbeth. The deed is committed with the fullest knowledge of its wickedness, and, indeed, of its folly. Macbeth knows, until the moment when his judgement is overpowered by his wife, that, whether or not there is retribution in the life to come, some crimes are so outrageous that they cannot escape vengeance here. Macbeth himself analyses for us the nature of his deed: it defies the ties of blood and loyalty, the trust between man and man on which society is built, the primitive sacredness of the guest, and the reverence that is due to virtue and innocence. Macbeth knows that the act is inhuman, that it does not 'become a man'. Lady Macbeth knows this too: she knows the deed is a violation of her womanhood; she must become 'unsexed', become a monster to do it.

The close of *Macbeth* shows the same deadly ironic justice as the close of *Dr. Faustus*. Macbeth and his wife expel pity and remorse from their natures, and they find themselves confronted by a world that has no pity for them. In the last act, nobody says a word of Macbeth that is not inspired by a cold hatred. He is 'this dead butcher', and he is allowed no death speech of exculpation. There is no restoration of the original image of the hero in this play as there is in *Othello*. To point the full horror of his hunting down we are shown, just before, the death of Young Siward, 'God's soldier'. For as Faustus is shown to us first and last in his study, so Macbeth is shown first and last as a soldier, and Young Siward's is the death he might have died. Macbeth did more than 'does become a man' and becomes, as he himself knew he would, 'none'. At the end of the play he is simply a wild beast to be destroyed. 'Turn, hell-hound, turn', cries Macduff to him, and he himself compares himself to a baited bear. His head is borne in like a monster's. He put aside feeling and he finds himself at the end incapable of feeling. He threw away 'golden opinions' and he gets curses; he broke the laws of hospitality and friendship, and he finds himself solitary in a world united against him.

Just as Shakespeare blackened the deed, so he refused to Macbeth any satisfactions upon earth. The ten years of just and prosperous reign in Holinshed are suppressed. The first words we hear Macbeth utter when we see him alone after his crowning are: 'To be thus is nothing.' The great central scene of the play impresses this on us by a vivid visual image: Macbeth wears the crown, but we do not see him seated among his lords; the murdered Banquo sits in his place. Like Faustus Macbeth desires incompatibles: he wants to overleap morality and law to achieve his ambition and at the same time to have the security that only obedience to the law can bring, the 'honour, love, obedience, troops of friends' which he realizes at the close he 'must not look to have'.

In both *Dr. Faustus* and *Macbeth* what astounds our imagination is the spectacle of the hero's suffering, the exploration of the nature of separation, intermittent in *Dr. Faustus*, but sustained throughout the play in *Macbeth*. Macbeth never loses that horror at himself which made him gaze upon his 'hangman's hands' as if they were not his. What he does is a perpetual offence to what he is, and he never ceases to feel it. The horror implicit in the exact Latin of Aquinas is here made vivid to the imagination: 'ideo non oportet, quamvis naturaliter inclinentur ad bonum, quod motus virtutis in eis sit, vel esse possit.'

At first sight *The Changeling* appears a very different play from either *Dr. Faustus* or *Macbeth*, though Beatrice-Joanna has sometimes been compared with Lady Macbeth because of the lack of imagination she shows when she incites to murder. The supernatural, which broods over *Macbeth* and is essential to the story of

Dr. Faustus, becomes here only a perfunctory acknowledgement of the popular taste for ghosts of murdered men. Beatrice-Joanna makes her choice and instigates to crime, prompted only by her passion for Alsemero, with no 'supernatural solicitings' to disturb her judgement. But though this is true literally, Middleton gains an effect that is beyond the natural by the wonderful invention of De Flores.[1]

The alterations that Middleton made in his source are very remarkable; all the play's most memorable situations are invented. The story as told by Reynolds is flat and pointless, as the following summary shows:[2]

The opening situation is the same as in the play: Beatrice-Joanna, who meets Alsemero at Mass by chance, is being urged by her father to marry Alonzo Piracquo. She has never liked Piracquo and is at once attracted by Alsemero. The story develops slowly with Beatrice-Joanna removed to the country, and corresponding clandestinely with Alsemero, who at last comes secretly to see her, admitted by her waiting woman, Diaphanta. Beatrice-Joanna tells him 'before *Piracquo* be in another World, there is no hope for *Alsemero* to inioy her for his wife in this'; whereupon Alsemero proposes to send him a challenge. But Beatrice-Joanna makes him promise not to meddle, and swears she can manage her father. The secret meeting is reported to her father, and she realizes that he is set upon her match with Piracquo, and so 'after shee had ruminated, and runne ouer many bloody designes: the diuell, who neuer flies from those that follow him, proffers her an inuention as execrable as damnable. There is a Gallant young Gentleman, of the Garrison of the Castle, who followes her father, that to her knowledge doth deeply honour, and dearely affect her: yea, she knowes, that at her request he will not sticke to murther *Piracquo*: his name is *Signiour Antonio de Flores*.'

Beatrice-Joanna then sends for de Flores and 'with many flattering smiles, and sugered speeches, acquaints him with her purpose and desire, making him many promises of kindenesse and courtesies'. De Flores is so 'intangled in the snares of her beautie, that hee freely promiseth to dispatch *Piracquo*; and so they first consult, and then agree vpon the manner how'. The murder is committed just as in the play, except that de Flores cuts off no finger for proof. He then tells Beatrice-Joanna what he has done, 'who doth heereat infinitely reioyce, and thankes him with many kisses'.

[1] Since the problem of authorship does not affect my argument, I use Middleton's name for brevity, instead of speaking of Middleton and Rowley.

[2] John Reynolds, *God's Revenge against Murder*, 1621, Book I, History IV, pp. 105–46.

Piracquo's disappearance is accepted as a mystery: Beatrice-Joanna hints to her lover that Piracquo is dead 'but in such palliating tearmes, that thereby shee may delude and carry away his iudgement, from imagining, that shee had the least shadow, or finger heerein'. Her father withdraws his objections and 'heere our two Louers, to their exceeding great content, and infinite ioy, are vnited, and by the bond of marriage of two persons made one'.

But after three happy months, Alsemero suddenly becomes jealous, and begins to restrain his wife's liberty. She complains to her father, but his remonstrances are useless, and Alsemero carries her off to the country. Her father sends de Flores to her with a letter, and de Flores 'salutes and kisseth her, with many amorous embracings and dalliances'. She bids him visit her often as her lover. Alsemero is told of the *liaison* by Diaphanta, and accuses Beatrice-Joanna of infidelity. She, 'in seeking to conceale her whoredome, must discouer her murther', and tells Alsemero that she has to show courtesy to de Flores, because he got rid of Piracquo for her. Alsemero, who is unaffected by the revelation of the murder, charges her to admit de Flores no more; but she continues with the affair, and being caught is killed with her paramour by Alsemero. At the trial Alsemero is acquitted of murder, when Diaphanta swears to the fact of adultery. But the author regards him as guilty of concealing the murder of Piracquo, and arranges a fit punishment for him too. He is challenged by Piracquo's younger brother, Tomaso, and by using treachery in the duel kills him. For this he is seized, and after confessing the truth is executed.

The power of Middleton's play lies in something which is quite absent from the source: the absolute contrast at the beginning and the identity at the close of Beatrice-Joanna and De Flores. She is young, beautiful, a virgin, and of secure rank; he is no 'Gallant young Gentleman', but a despised serving-man, an 'ominous ill-fac'd fellow', one of those broken soldiers of fortune who are so common in Jacobean tragedy, and he bears the marks of a dissolute life on his face. Middleton is usually praised and praised rightly for the intense realism of his characterization, and particularly for the two studies of Beatrice-Joanna and De Flores; but there is more than realism here. What Mephistophilis is to Faustus, what the 'supernatural solicitings' and the horror of the deed are to Macbeth, De Flores is to Beatrice-Joanna. He is repulsive and she has a strong instinctive loathing of him. She too sins against her nature, when she accepts the thing her nature most loathes as the instrument of her will. The deed comes to her mind through him, because she recognizes him as a suitable instrument. She is horrified when Alsemero suggests a challenge. She is afraid he may be killed, or that the law may step in and seize him. Her instinct tells her that he is an innocent man, and so she remembers another who is not:

> Blood-guiltiness becomes a fouler visage;—
> And now I think on one; I was to blame,
> I ha' marr'd so good a market with my scorn.[1]

It has been said that Beatrice-Joanna has no moral sense: that she is irresponsible, and only develops a sense of responsibility at the close of the play. This is true in a sense; but it might be truer to say that she develops a moral consciousness through her violation of what is fundamentally a moral instinct and a very deep one: the instinct which tells her that De Flores is her opposite.

Middleton's handling of the centre of his play is just as striking. In the centre of *Macbeth* we have the banquet, the concrete image of a hollow kingship; in the centre of *The Changeling* is the marriage that is no marriage. On her wedding night, Beatrice-Joanna has to send her waiting-woman to her husband's bed; we see her outside the door in a frenzy of jealousy and impatience. She too has given away her 'eternal jewel' and got nothing in exchange. The three months of happiness in the source have disappeared, as did the ten years of prosperous kingship in Holinshed. Beatrice-Joanna might say of her married state as Macbeth does of his kingship: 'To be thus is nothing.' She employs De Flores to get Alsemero. She loses Alsemero and gets De Flores. She becomes 'the deed's creature'. In the end she recognizes her link with him and what she has become, and sees herself as defiled and defiling. Like Faustus, who continues to affirm his bargain, like Macbeth who adds murder to murder, she too is involved in repetition of the original act; she has again to employ De Flores for her safety; he becomes to her 'a wondrous necessary man' and she comments: 'Here's a man worth loving', as he makes his preparations for the dispatch of Diaphanta.

With the same sense of the implications of his theme, Middleton makes Alsemero absolutely innocent of any complicity. Beatrice-Joanna and De Flores tower over the play, as Macbeth and Lady Macbeth, and Faustus and Mephistophilis do. Alsemero's function

---

[1] Quotations from *The Changeling* are from *The Works of Thomas Middleton* edited by A. H. Bullen, 1885–6, vol. vi.

is not to interest us in himself, but to be a standard by which we see what has happened to Beatrice-Joanna. He was to be her reward, and so, in an ironic sense, he is, when he turns upon her with horror and cries: 'O, thou art all deform'd!' She makes a last despairing effort with a lie: 'Remember, I am true unto your bed'; to which Alsemero replies:

> The bed itself's a charnel, the sheets shrouds
> For murder'd carcasses.

At last she tells the truth, and the truth of the play emerges.

Beatrice-Joanna.   Alsemero, I'm a stranger to your bed;
　　　　　　　　　　Your bed was cozen'd on the nuptial night,
　　　　　　　　　　For which your false bride died.

De Flores.   Yes, and the while I coupled with your mate
　　　　　　　At barley break; now we are left in hell.

Vermandero.   We are all there, it circumscribes us here.[1]

It is not suggested that there is any direct relation between these three plays, in the sense that one was inspired by the others; nor is it suggested that when Milton drew his Satan he had these great tragic figures in mind. What is suggested is that Satan belongs to their company, and if we ask where the idea of damnation was handled with seriousness and intensity in English literature before Milton, we can only reply: on the tragic stage. Satan is, of course, a character in an epic, and he is in no sense the hero of the epic as a whole. But he is a figure of heroic magnitude and heroic energy, and he is developed by Milton with dramatic emphasis and dramatic intensity. He is shown, to begin with, engaged in heroic and stupendous enterprises, and again and again in moments of dramatic clash; rousing his supine followers, awaiting his moment in the great debate, confronted with Sin and Death and Chaos itself, flinging taunt for taunt at his angelic adversaries. But, most strikingly, he is presented to us by the means by which the great Elizabethan dramatists commended their tragic heroes to our hearts and imaginations: by soliloquy. Milton gives to Satan no less than five long soliloquies

---

[1] The echo from *Dr. Faustus* can hardly be accidental.

> Hell hath no limits, nor is circumscrib'd
> In one self place; but where we are is hell,
> And where hell is, there must we ever be.

in Eden, three in the fourth book and two in the ninth.[1] In them he reveals to us 'the hot Hell that alwayes in him burnes', and recalls again and again

> the bitter memorie
> Of what he was, what is, and what must be
> Worse.

It is in them that the quality which makes Satan a tragic figure appears most strikingly, and it is the quality that Mr. Lewis makes weightiest against him: his egoism.

'Satan's monomaniac concern with himself and his supposed rights and wrongs is a necessity of the Satanic predicament', says Mr. Lewis. The same is true of the great tragic heroes of Shakespeare, and this capacity of theirs to expose relentlessly the full horror of their situations is just what makes them the heroes of their plays.[2] The predicament of Claudius is direr than Hamlet's but Shakespeare pays little attention to it; Malcolm is the righteous avenger of a horrible crime, but the sympathy we feel for him we take for granted. We are held enthralled instead by the voice of Hamlet, defining for us his 'bad dreams', or that of Macbeth telling us of solitude. If we are to complain that wherever he goes, and whatever he sees, Satan finds nothing of interest but himself, and to compare him unfavourably with Adam, who can converse on topics of general

---

[1] In spite of the explanatory and anticipatory element in these soliloquies, their general effect, particularly in the two longest, IV. 32–113 and IX. 99–178, is quite different from the effect of the soliloquies of villains such as Richard III or Iago. In them we are conscious of activity of intellect and atrophy of feeling; here, as in the soliloquies of Hamlet or Macbeth, the plans announced are less important than the analysis of the hero's predicament.

[2] Henry James puts this well in the preface to *The Princess Casamassima*, London, 1921, p. viii. 'This in fact I have ever found rather terribly the point— that the figures in any picture, the agents in any drama, are interesting only in proportion as they feel their respective situations; since the consciousness, on their part, of the complication exhibited forms for us their link of connection with it. But there are degrees of feeling—the muffled, the faint, the just sufficient, the barely intelligent, as we may say; and the acute, the intense, the complete, in a word—the power to be finely aware and richly responsible. It is those moved in this latter fashion who "get most" out of all that happens to them and who in so doing enable us, as readers of their record, as participators by a fond attention, also to get most. Their being finely aware—as Hamlet and Lear, say, are finely aware—*makes* absolutely the intensity of their adventure, gives the maximum of sense to what befalls them.'

interest such as the stars, what should we say of Lear, who finds in the majesty of the storm or the misery of the naked beggarman only fresh incentives to talk about the unkindness of his daughters? If we can say of a speech of Satan's that 'it fails to be roaring farce only because it spells agony', we can say the same of Macbeth, complaining at the close of a career of murderous egoism that he has no friends, or of Beatrice-Joanna, 'a woman dipp'd in blood', talking of modesty. Satan is an egoist and Satan is a comic character in exactly the same way as Hamlet, Macbeth, Othello, and Lear are egoists and comic characters. 'O gull! O dolt!' cries Emilia to Othello. We do not pity him the less because we assent.

The critical problem of *Paradise Lost* seems to me to lie here. We are concerned with Satan in a way that is quite different from the way we are concerned with Adam and Eve. In Mr. Lewis's treatment this is quite clear. He uses all his skill to make us regard Satan as a despicable human being, discussing him in terms of 'children, film-stars, politicians, or minor poets'; but he uses equal skill to make us realize we must not regard Adam in this way. If he is right, as I think he is, in pressing a distinction between our attitudes to the two figures, he poses an acute problem for the reader of *Paradise Lost*, and appears to convict Milton of the artistic failure involved in a mixture of kinds.

The distinction I feel I would express in rather different terms. Adam and Eve are representative figures, and the act they perform is a great symbolic act. The plucking of the apple is not in itself imaginatively powerful; its power over us springs from its very triviality; the meaning and the consequences are so much greater than the image of a hand stretched out to pluck the fruit. The temptation and fall of Eve is profound in its psychological analysis, but it lacks the shock of dramatic situation. As Mr. Lewis says: 'The whole thing is so quick, each new element of folly, malice, and corruption enters so unobtrusively, so naturally, that it is hard to realize we have been watching the genesis of murder. We expect something more like Lady Macbeth's "unsex me here".' In other words, the situation is not dramatically exploited, lingered on. The scenes between Adam and Eve are deeply human, but they lack the terror, and the dreadful exaggeration, of tragedy. The quarrel is only too sadly lifelike, but it does not appal us, as does the spectacle of Othello's striking Desdemona. In the ninth book and the books that follow, Milton is tracing with insight, with humanity, and with humility the process in man through sin to repentance. The progress is steady and ordered; what is said is fully adequate to the situation, appropriate but not astounding. But Satan's defiance of God is not expressed by a symbolic gesture; in his rebellion the act and its meaning are one. And in the earlier books, and indeed wherever Satan appears, what is said goes beyond the necessities of the narrative, because Milton was writing as a tragic artist obsessed by his imagination of a particular experience, and exploring it with the maximum intensity. The experience might be called 'exclusion'. Wherever he goes, whatever he looks at, Satan is perpetually conscious of this. His exclusion is self-willed, as is the exclusion of Faustus, Macbeth, and Beatrice-Joanna. Like them he gazes on a heaven he cannot enter; like them he is in the end deformed; like them he remains in the memory with all the stubborn objectivity of the tragic.

If it can be accepted that Satan as he is conceived and presented to us is a tragic figure, it is possible to suggest another explanation for the Romantic misconception of the poem than a dislike of Milton's theology. The early nineteenth century was greatly concerned, it would seem, with tragic experience; its great poets wanted to be 'miserable and mighty poets of the human heart'. All of them attempted to write tragedy, but, with the possible exception of *The Cenci*, they produced nothing that is admitted to be fully tragic. It was also a period remarkable for penetrating and subtle Shakespearian criticism, but for a criticism which lost a sense of the play in its discussion of the psychology of the characters, and which tended to minimize in the tragic heroes the very thing that made them tragic and not pathetic, the evil in them. In the criticism of the period Hamlet is 'a sweet prince', Lear 'a man more sinned against than sinning'. Hamlet's savagery and Lear's appalling rages are overlooked. Lamb turned from the stage because he could not bear the cruel comedy of *King Lear*, or the sight of Desdemona in Othello's arms. Realized intensely in the mind, divorced from his action in the play, the tragic hero was reshaped. It is of the essence of tragedy that it forces us to look at what we normally do not care to look at, and have not invented for ourselves.[1] The failure either

[1] It may be suggested that the success of *The Cenci*, compared with other tragedies of the period, is partly due to the fact that the story was not invented by

to write or to appreciate tragedy in the Romantic period springs from the same cause: the Romantic poets' preoccupation with themselves, and their lack of capacity to submit themselves to the 'mystery of things'. The famous passage in which Keats defined Shakespeare's quality as 'Negative Capability' goes to the root of the matter. But 'Negative Capability' is as necessary to the spectator and critic of tragedy as to its creator. The tragic is destroyed when we identify the hero with ourselves. Just as the Romantic critics tended to see the heroes of Shakespeare's tragedies as more admirable, more tender, more purely pathetic than they are, so feeling Satan's kinship with the tragic hero they sentimentalized him and made him conform to their limited conception of tragedy. Because he was to be pitied, they minimized the evil in him, inventing wrongs to explain and excuse it.[1]

The present age is also not an age of great tragic writing, though there are some signs of a revival of the tragic spirit. Its best poetry is symbolic, and its criticism, in reviving for us the medieval tradition of allegory, tends towards an allegorical interpretation of all art. Mr.

Shelley. He plainly felt some of the 'superstitious horror' which he tells us the story still aroused in Italy, and was fascinated by the portrait of Beatrice.

[1] In the preface to *Prometheus Unbound*, Shelley compared Satan with Prometheus and declared that Prometheus is the 'more poetical character' since he is 'exempt from the taints of ambition, envy, revenge, and a desire for personal aggrandisement, which, in the Hero of *Paradise Lost*, interfere with the interest'. He thought that the character of Satan 'engenders in the mind a pernicious casuistry which leads us to weigh his faults with his wrongs, and to excuse the former because the latter exceed all measure'. When he wrote the preface to *The Cenci* Shelley had abandoned the notion that moral perfection made a character poetically interesting, and acknowledged that if Beatrice had been 'wise and better' she would not have been a tragic character, but he speaks again of the 'casuistry' by which we try to justify what she does, while feeling that it needs justification. When he compared Milton's God and his Devil in *A Defence of Poetry*, Shelley declared Satan was morally superior on the grounds that his situation and his wrongs excused in him the revengefulness which is hateful in his triumphant Adversary. In all three passages one can see Shelley's feeling that the Hero is a person whose side we take. The theme of a nature warped by suffering injustice, and repaying crime with crime, is certainly tragic when handled with seriousness and moral integrity as in *The Cenci*, though it slides all too easily into the sentimental absurdities of the Byronic outcast, and it is always in danger of shallowness. It is the tragic formula of an age which does not believe in original sin, and thinks of evil as not bred in the heart, but caused by circumstances.

Lewis, in exposing Shelley's misconceptions, has inverted the Romantic attitude, for the effect of his chapter on Satan is to make us feel that because Satan is wicked and wicked with no excuse, he is not to be pitied, but is to be hated and despised. Shelley saw in Satan the indomitable rebel against unjust tyranny, and while regretting the 'taints' in his character excused them. Mr. Lewis, who thinks more harshly of himself and of human nature than Shelley did, exposes Satan with all the energy and argumentative zeal which we used to hear our European Service employing in denouncing the lies of Goebbels and revealing the true nature of the promises of Hitler. Both Shelley's passionate sympathy and Mr. Lewis's invective derive from the same fundamental attitude: 'It is we who are Satan.' As often happens with plural statements, this is a merely verbal extension of the singular; that is to say, it is infected by an egoism that distorts the proper function of the tragic. When we contemplate the lost Archangel, we should not be seeing ourselves in heroic postures defying tyrants, nor weighing up our chances of ending in Hell, any more than, while we watch the progress of Lear, we should be thinking how ungrateful other people are to us for our goodness to them, or resolving to think before we speak next time. Though Shelley and Mr. Lewis are on different sides, they agree in taking sides. Neither of them accepts the complexity of the emotion which Satan arouses.

The tragic is something outside ourselves which we contemplate with awe and pity. Aristotle began the perversion of tragic theory when he suggested that the terror we feel is a terror that the same fate may befall us. Aristotle was a philosopher and a moralist, and, like many of his kind since, wanted to make tragedy safe and useful. But tragedy does not exist to provide us with horrid warnings. 'Pity', said Stephen Dedalus, expanding the cryptic Aristotelian formula, 'is the feeling which arrests the mind in the presence of whatsoever is grave and constant in human sufferings and unites it with the human sufferer. Terror is the feeling which arrests the mind in the presence of whatsoever is grave and constant in human sufferings and unites it with the secret cause.'[1] We accept the justice by which the tragic hero is destroyed. Indeed, if it were not for the justice we should have no pity for him. The acceptance of the justice makes possible the pity, and the pity calls for the justice without which it

[1] James Joyce, *A Portrait of the Artist as a Young Man*, chapter v.

would turn to loathing. But the cause must be secret in tragedy; it must be felt within the facts exposed; what is hateful in the tragic world is that Eternal Law should argue.

The unity of tragedy is destroyed if the critic makes himself either the champion of the hero or the advocate of Eternal Law. Tragedy 'arrests the mind' as the sufferings of others do, but as our own do not. But in life the arrest is short, for we are involved in the necessity of action. As spectators of tragedy we are released from our perpetual burden of asking ourselves what we ought to do. To use tragedy either as a moral example or as a moral warning is to destroy the glory of tragedy, the power it has to release us from ourselves by arousing in us the sense of magnitude and the sense of awe. Wordsworth, the most untragic of great poets, saw something of the nature of tragedy when he wrote,

> Suffering is permanent, obscure and dark,
> And shares the nature of infinity.

Tragedy may present us with a 'false infinite', but it has that nature. It is permanent 'with such permanence as time has'. Like the rock in T. S. Eliot's *The Dry Salvages*,

> Waves wash over it, fogs conceal it;
> On a halcyon day it is merely a monument,
> In navigable weather it is always a seamark
> To lay a sudden course by: but in the sombre season
> Or the sudden fury, is what it always was.

The figure of Satan has this imperishable significance. If he is not the heroic rebel of Shelley's imagination, neither is he merely an 'unerring picture of the "sense of injur'd merit" in its actual operations upon character'.

But if Mr. Lewis's view seems like an inversion of Shelley's, Mr. Williams's is not very unlike Blake's. What Blake perceived in *Paradise Lost* was a radical dualism, which was perhaps the inevitable effect of treating the myth in epic form. Among the many difficulties inherent in the subject was the difficulty of knowing how much to include in the direct action and how much to put into relations. It was impossible for Milton to begin where his tragedy *Adam Unparadised* was to have begun, in Paradise; the direct action would have been insufficient to fill the epic form. Even as it is,

Paradise Lost is overweighted with relations. Epic tradition forbade him to begin at the beginning with the exaltation of the Son. Possibly his decision to begin with the moment when Satan lifts his head from the burning waves was inevitable once he had decided against the dramatic form in which he first conceived the subject. But the effect of beginning there, and of the whole of the 'Prologue in Hell', is to make the action of the poem seem to originate in Hell, and to make the acts of Heaven seem only the response called out by the energies of Hell. However much Milton contradicts this later and asserts the overriding Will, the structure and design of his poem contradict and fight against his intention. The parallel, so often praised, between the silence in Hell and the silence in Heaven reinforces the feeling of dualism, since *contraria sunt aequalia*, and Satan and the Son seem balanced against each other, as Blake saw them to be, while the priority of the scene in Hell seems to make Heaven parody Hell rather than Hell Heaven. Mr. Williams's statement that 'the Son is the Image of Derivation in Love, and Satan is the Image of personal clamour for personal independence' is not unlike Blake's assertion of 'the contraries from which spring what the religious call good and evil'. It suggests at least that Milton made Satan too important in the scheme of his poem.

Perhaps the problem which *Paradise Lost* presents to the critic has its origin in Milton's own change of mind over the form in which he was to write his masterpiece. He first chose the subject of the Fall of Man as suited to a tragedy, and we know that he not only planned the disposition of his material in dramatic form, but actually began the writing. His draft *Adam Unparadised* provides Lucifer with two soliloquies: in the first he was to 'bemoan himself' and 'seek revenge upon man'; in the second he was to appear 'relating and consulting on what he had done to the destruction of man'. The first soliloquy was therefore to have been mainly expository, and in the second Lucifer was to take over the duty of the classical messenger and relate the catastrophe. The strict concentration of classical tragedy would have prevented Lucifer from usurping on the main interest, and his predicament, however much he 'bemoaned himself', would have been subordinated to the whole design. Why Milton changed his mind we do not know, and he set himself a problem of extraordinary difficulty in choosing to treat this particular subject in epic form. He had somehow to fill the large epic structure, and it is difficult to see how else he could have done it than by expanding Satan's role. But it is possible that he turned away from tragedy because his interest had radiated out from the true centre of the action, the Fall itself, and his imagination demanded the larger freedom of the epic. Certainly the fact that Phillips remembered seeing the opening lines of Satan's first soliloquy as part of the projected tragedy suggests that Milton's conception of Satan began to form early, and it may have been that the writing of this first soliloquy showed Milton that the tragic form would not allow him to develop his conception as fully as he wished to. But whether the decision to begin his poem with Satan in Hell was simply the inevitable result of enlarging his action to make it sufficient for an epic, or whether it was Milton's interest in Satan that led him to abandon tragedy for epic, and he therefore naturally began with Satan, the figure of Satan, originally conceived dramatically, is developed dramatically throughout, and Milton expended his creative energies and his full imaginative power in exploring the fact of perversity within a single heroic figure. In this, as in much else, he is what we loosely call an Elizabethan, sacrificing simplicity of effect and strength of design to imaginative opportunity; creating the last great tragic figure in our literature and destroying the unity of his poem in doing so. The dualism which Blake found in the poem's thought, and which in Mr. Williams's analysis seems to dictate its design, is certainly there in its manner. The strong emotions of pity and terror do not mix well with the interest, sympathy, and 'admiration' which we feel for the heroes of what Mr. Lewis has called 'the secondary epic', and, with the possible exception of Hazlitt, no critic of note has done justice to both Satan and Adam as artistic creations. The subject demanded an 'infernal Serpent'; instead Milton has given us 'a lost Archangel'. There would be no difficulty if Satan were simply an Iago; the difficulty arises because he is a Macbeth.[1]

[1] I reprint this essay as it was originally written, though it will be obvious that I have moved away from the position I held when I wrote it. I am now arguing that the strength of Milton's design holds together the cosmic and the human theme, and that it is the glory of *Paradise Lost* that it contains both the tragic figure of the 'lost Archangel' and the human figures of Adam and Eve: what astounds our imaginations and what touches our experience, the *mysterium iniquitatis* and the frailty of man and woman.

APPENDIX B

Milton's First Illustrator[1]

In 1688 Jacob Tonson, who soon after the beginning of his career as a publisher had been fortunate and wise enough to acquire half the copyright of *Paradise Lost*,[2] brought out, with the aid of an impressive list of subscribers, the fourth edition of Milton's epic, in a form worthy of the English Virgil. This was a handsome volume in folio, finely printed and 'Adorn'd with Sculptures'. These illustrations have not received much attention from students of the poem, and if they are referred to at all it is usually in a slighting tone. Such neglect is not wholly deserved. John Baptist Medina, who supplied eleven out of the twelve designs,[3] was not without talent, and he was either a careful reader of the poem himself, or was carefully directed by someone else. He made, whether by himself or under guidance, a genuine attempt at interpretation. Since he was fifteen years old when Milton died and produced his designs only fourteen years later, they may be regarded as almost the work of a contemporary. I believe there is some interest in seeing how a man of the late seventeenth century read the poem, what episodes seemed to him significant, and how he attempted to solve the problems presented by the vast range and variety of Milton's Christian epic.

Medina was a Spaniard, who had been trained in Brussels, a pupil of François Duchatel. He came to London in 1686, but soon migrated northwards, and from 1688 settled in Edinburgh, where he carried on a large practice as a portrait painter. He had been trained in historical painting, but soon declined into being a 'painter of faces', and was so successful that he gained the title of 'the Kneller of the North'. His illustrations to *Paradise Lost* are his only

[1] Reprinted from *Essays and Studies*, 1956.

[2] He became sole owner in 1690 and, according to Spence, said that he made more by *Paradise Lost* than by any other poem. See A. W. Pollard, 'The Bibliography of Milton', *The Library*, New Series, x, 1909.

[3] The illustration to Book IV is ascribed to Bernard Lens the elder. Although Medina's name does not appear on the plates for Books I, II, VIII, and XII, they are plainly by the same hand as the remaining plates which are ascribed to him.

surviving works which are not portraits; but, according to Vertue, he also designed engravings to Ovid's *Metamorphoses*, although these were not engraved.¹ It is not strange that Tonson turned to a young foreigner to carry out his ambitious scheme of issuing Milton's poem in a form comparable to that of the fine illustrated Virgil of 1654, for at the close of the seventeenth century a British school of history painting hardly existed.² Indeed, when Tonson came to publish Dryden's Virgil nine years later, he did not commission fresh illustrations, but was content to adapt the old ones from Ogilby's.³

Medina's first problem was to decide on his method.⁴ There were two possibilities. He might, like the illustrators of Ariosto, use the old method of Biblical illustration and make one comprehensive design for each book, giving the various episodes in sequence beginning at the bottom of the page and continuing in a zigzag to the top. Or he might, like the illustrators to Ogilby's Virgil, the most impressive example of an illustrated poem in England at this date, choose a single episode and make a picture of it: the method of a modern illustrator. He seems to have decided that neither method did full justice to his text, and he compromised. At first sight, particularly in the first books, he appears to have followed the second method, and to have chosen his episode and portrayed it as dramatically as possible; but, as one looks at the picture, one recognizes that he had used subsidiary episodes from the book to fill in his background; so that, while a single dramatic moment is well rendered by the main design, the richness of the book is not left unrepresented,

---

¹ *Vertue Notebooks*, Walpole Society, xviii. 48 and 46; J. Caw, *Scottish Painting*, 1908, pp. 20, 21.

² Vertue says of Medina that he 'would have made a good history painter had he liv'd were suitable encouragement was to be mett with'.

³ Some alterations were made from the illustrations which had appeared in 1654 and 1668. The nose of Æneas is more Roman and 'sometimes he bears also something like the wig of King William; a circumstance which must have given additional point to certain malign allusions in Dryden's preface: "Æneas though he married the heiress of the crown, yet claimed no title to it during the life of his father-in-law".' W. P. Ker, *Essays of John Dryden*, 1926, vol. i, p. lxx.

⁴ It seems likely, since he was a foreigner and had only been in England a very short time when Tonson commissioned him, that Medina was assisted in reading the poem and in choosing episodes; but for convenience I speak of 'Medina', although he probably did not work independently and the choice of incidents may be Tonson's or someone else's.

Illustration to Book I of *Paradise Lost*
by John Baptist Medina (1688)

but can be found in the background. But although this describes his method generally, he varied it according to the nature of the book he was illustrating, and his treatment of Book IX, for instance, is very different from his treatment of Books I and II. It is here that the interest of Medina's attempt lies; and to study his designs leads once more to the recognition of the extreme originality of Milton. For Medina, like his poet, was a trained classical artist, skilled in the use of conventions, with a wide range of conventional figures and types to hand; but he had to change and modify these conventions to suit his author as no illustrator of Virgil would have needed to do. The illustrations to Ogilby's Virgil, charming as they are, and penetrated with Renaissance classical feeling, are simply historical paintings; but Medina, faced with the Miltonic Heaven, Hell, and Paradise, and their inhabitants, had to draw on a wide range of types, and had to vary his types and his style from book to book.

This variety in treatment and the careful reading of the poem which is apparent in some of the illustrations can best be displayed by an account of the plates, which will also show that Medina was not unskilful in his choice of episodes. For Book I he chose the moment when Satan 'rears from off the Pool his mighty Stature' (I. 221–2). The foreground is occupied by the huge forms of the rebel angels 'rowling in the fiery Gulfe' (I. 52); in the background

the flames
Drivn backward slope their pointing spires, & rowld
In billows, leave i' th' midst a horrid Vale. (I. 222–4.)

In the far distance, on the left, is Pandaemonium, with a token assembly of the 'thousand Demy-Gods on golden seat's' (I. 796). In Book II Medina chose the scene at the Gates of Hell, the meeting of Satan with Sin and Death, and did not attempt to include any subsidiary episodes. It must be owned that this is a far less impressive picture than the first. The shattered door on which Satan stands suggests a careless reading of the poem, and the three strange flying creatures at the top of the page seem to be due to some odd flight of fancy remote from the text. Death, also, is not the shadowy, formless horror of Milton's imagination, but the stereotyped image of the skeleton, familiar from the old Dance of Death blocks. The representation of Sin, 'the Snakie Sorceress', is literal, but can hardly be called successful. She appears as a Peter Lely beauty, emerging from a tangled heap of serpents and monsters, but her open mouth, ready to intervene with 'hideous outcry', gives her an unfortunately vacant expression.

By contrast the episode from Book III is both finely chosen and finely conceived and executed. It portrays the moment when Milton turns from the glorious company of Heaven to the single figure of the Adversary:

> Thus they in Heav'n, above the starry Sphear,
> Thir happie hours in joy and hymning spent,
> Mean while upon the firm opacous Globe
> Of this round World, whose first convex divides
> The luminous inferior Orbs, enclos'd
> From *Chaos* and th' inroad of Darkness old,
> *Satan* alighted walks.   (III. 416–22.)

The upper part of the page is occupied by the figure of Christ seated on a cloud: He is surrounded by angels, those on His right bearing a large cross, held slantwise behind His outstretched arm and nimbus, those on His left bearing harps. A beam of light streams down from Him on to the figure of Satan, who stands alone on the outer shell of the universe. The composition is striking; and the introduction of the symbol of the Cross at this moment, just after the Messiah has 'offerd himself to die for mans offence' (III. 409), with the contrast between the happy company of Heaven and the lonely figure of Satan, shows a real appreciation of the significance of the book. The whole pose of Satan expresses 'his sad exclusion from the dores of Bliss' (III. 525). The background is filled in with the landscape of Paradise; on the left side of the picture the tiny figure of Satan, as a stripling cherub, is seen flying towards the Angel in the Sun, while below, in the form of a devil, he is shown on a mount gazing down upon Adam and Eve in Paradise. We can forgive Medina for making Satan see Uriel while he is flying towards the sun; he could hardly have represented their meeting on the great Orb itself. His anticipation of Satan's first sight of Adam and Eve was probably suggested to him by Uriel's closing words to the disguised Satan:

> That spot to which I point is *Paradise*,
> *Adams* abode, those loftie shades his Bowre.   (III. 733–4.)

Illustration to Book III of *Paradise Lost*
by John Baptist Medina (1688)

For some reason Medina did not provide the illustration to Book
IV, which is the work of Bernard Lens. It at once strikes the eye as
less effective and more archaic than the three previous plates. The
treatment is episodic, and the main design does not stand out clearly.
On the left-hand side is the eastern gate of Paradise, the 'Rock of
Alabaster' (IV. 543), and before it sits Gabriel with three other
angels, their 'Celestial Armourie' (IV. 553) hanging behind them.
Towards them Uriel descends 'gliding through the Eeven on a Sun
beam' (IV. 555). The background is filled with the doings of Adam
and Eve; above, on the right, they are being amused by the antics
of the animals, including the elephant, who though not actually
wreathing 'his lithe Proboscis' seems to be very conscious of it,
while, on the Tree of Life, looking down on them, Satan sits in the
shape of a cormorant. In the centre they are praying with lifted
hands before they retire to their bower, and in the right-hand corner
they are asleep in the bower, and Satan, in the shape of a toad, is
squatting 'close at the eare of *Eve*' (IV. 800), about to be prodded
by the spears of Ithuriel and Zephon. The sky is adorned with the
Zodiac, showing the sign of the Scales (IV. 997), and the further
background shows the Angelic squadron,

> With ported Spears, as thick as when a field
> Of *Ceres* ripe for harvest waving bends
> Her bearded Grove of ears. (IV. 980–2.)

There is an unsophisticated charm in this crowded design with its
comic animals and ill-drawn little figures, but it has little merit in
itself or as an interpretation of the book.

For Book V Medina has also used the episodic manner, but with
far greater skill. In the foreground Adam and Eve kneel in prayer
at the door of their bower. On the left, further back, Adam stands
looking up to watch the descent of Raphael, whose flying form
dominates the page; in the background, Adam greets Raphael at the
door of the bower, and Eve prepares a meal of fruit. But for Book
VI he has reverted to the manner of Book I, and has chosen a single
episode; the moment of the rout of the rebel angels at the appearance
of the Messiah. The good angels are standing firm on their cloud on
the left of the page; the rebel angels are toppling off theirs on the
right. They are falling into the burning lake of Hell, whose dismal
light reflects upon them. In the centre is the Messiah in the Chariot

of Paternal Deity. Medina has made little attempt to represent this mystical vehicle or its escort. He has been content to show the Messiah as a Roman-conqueror, seated on a car and convoyed by four cherubs with the normal complement of faces. For some reason which I cannot explain, in the middle of the burning lake of Hell, he has placed Leviathan spouting. I have wondered whether the whale is a rationalization of the familiar yawning mouth in medieval representations of Hell. However that may be, the whale is inaccurately represented, as in the pictures of Jonah and others of which Sir Thomas Browne complained, where 'Whales are described with two prominent spouts on their heads; whereas indeed they have but one in the forehead, and terminating over the windpipe'.[1] After this, the design of Book VII is rather dull; it shows Adam listening to Raphael's discourse and Eve on the point of withdrawing, while above, in four medallions, four of the days of creation are shown. Book VIII, on the contrary, has a charming illustration. In the foreground Adam sits, alone in Paradise. But for the lack of an open shirt, he looks curiously like Lord Byron. He is surrounded by creatures, birds and beasts, including a pensive unicorn, but his loneliness is apparent. In the background he is seen rising from sleep to behold the newly created Eve. Behind, Eve is shown gardening and also resting from the heat, and in the far background Adam says farewell to the affable Archangel. With the exception of the illustration to Book VI, these centre plates have a quiet and undramatic manner that is well suited to the matter and style of the middle books of the poem.

When we come to Book IX, the climax of the poem, there is a striking change of atmosphere, but Medina does not return to the heroic and dramatic manner of the first three plates. He apparently felt that this book, for all its incidental dramatic power, is essentially narrative, and that he could not illustrate it adequately by selecting a single episode. So he tells the whole story in its stages. In the right-hand corner Satan gazes down with fascination and repugnance on a huge coiled serpent. Occupying as they do the foreground, these two dark figures, by their position and the scale they are drawn on, give a sinister impression to the whole plate, which might otherwise, from its episodic handling, appear trivial. Behind them, on the left, Adam and Eve are discussing their morning's tasks, and in the centre

---

[1] *Pseudodoxia Epidemica*, v. 19.

Illustration to Book IX of *Paradise Lost*
by John Baptist Medina (1688)

they are parting with somewhat petulant gestures. In the further distance, on the right, is the Tree, with Eve eating the apple, and the serpent standing before her like a corkscrew on its point. Towards the centre, still further back, Eve is handing the apple to Adam, and beyond, on the left, they both stand girdled with figleaves, while above them lightening flashes and a huge black cloud has gathered:

> Skie lowr'd, and muttering Thunder, som sad drops
> Wept at compleating of the mortal Sin
> Original.   (IX. 1002–4.)

In Book X Medina comes nearer to the manner of the earlier books. The top half of the page is filled by the guardian Angels, flying back to Heaven:

> Up into Heav'n from Paradise in hast
> Th' Angelic Guards ascended, mute and sad.   (X. 17–18.)

Beneath, in the left-hand corner, Adam lies, repelling the penitent Eve, who kneels by him. These figures make up the main design and express well the despair on earth and the breach in the familiar intercourse of men and angels which resulted from the Fall. In the middle distance Satan is greeting Sin and Death; Sin is now without her loathsome progeny, and appears as 'his faire inchanting Daughter' (X. 352). Behind them is the 'ridge of pendent Rock over the vext Abyss' (X. 313–14), and, in the far distance, Satan is relating the story of his success to the assembled demons in Pandaemonium. Behind them rises the 'shew of the forbidden Tree', up which they swarm in the form of serpents.

The illustration to Book XI is even more in the manner of the earlier books. It shows the coming of Michael, who is drawn exactly as Milton describes him,

> Not in shape Celestial, but as man
> Clad to meet Man.   (XI. 239–40.)

He wears the 'militarie Vest' over his arms; his helmet is unbuckled, his sword hangs by his side, and his spear is in his hand (XI. 241–8). He confronts Adam with authority, and Adam's pose expresses penitence and submission, though Eve, who is leaning on a bank behind Adam, is less successfully portrayed. In the background, Eve lies asleep at the foot of the Hill of Vision, while Adam stands with Michael on the summit. The rest of the background is finely filled in with the 'Signs, imprest on Bird, Beast, Aire' (XI. 182). The sky is lowering, the eagle, the 'Bird of *Jove*, stoopt from his aerie tour' is driving before him 'two Birds of gayest plume'; the lion is pursuing 'down from a Hill'

> a gentle brace,
> Goodliest of all the Forrest, Hart and Hinde.   (XI. 188–9.)

After this careful and imaginative treatment of Book XI the handling of Book XII is a sad disappointment. As with Book II, Medina chose a single episode: Adam and Eve being escorted from Paradise. They are descending what looks like a subway, pushed by Michael, who carries a wavy sword. These steps, surrounded by angels floating on clouds, are a sadly tame rendering of

> the Gate
> With dreadful Faces throng'd and fiery Armes:

and Adam and Eve are not even 'hand in hand'. No attempt has been made to suggest what is so moving in Milton's final picture: the mutual love, and humble faith and hope, with which the parents of the human race set out upon the great adventure of human history. The reason is that the subject of the Expulsion from Paradise was too familiar; and Medina, instead of studying his author, was content with a bad imitation of Raphael's 'Expulsion' in the Loggia, itself derived from Masaccio's fresco in the Carmine at Florence. All he did was to take a standard, hackneyed design and add some angels on clouds at the top.

The interest of the illustrations to the student of Milton lies, I think, in two things. First, if we recognize, as I hope this rather lengthy account has shown, that Medina was making a serious attempt to illustrate and interpret and not merely to decorate the poem, and that he had studied it with some care, as his use of detail shows, we must be struck by the variety of treatment he found necessary. He began by employing a heroic and dramatic manner, which he used for the first three books, and he recurred to this manner when he came to the War in Heaven in Book VI and, unsuccessfully, in Book XII. But he not only abandoned it in the middle books, where the text indeed gave him little opportunity for using it; he also seems to have felt it was unsuitable for Books IX and X, the climax of the poem, containing the main action of the epic. Medina's illustrations suggest to us that even in the seventeenth century a discriminating reader felt a difference of style and treatment between the first books of *Paradise Lost* and the remainder of the poem, and while he might not have agreed with some later critics in rating the first books more highly, at least he would have agreed that they affected his imagination differently. He appears to have felt deeply the contrast between the magnitude of the subject and treatment in the first three books, and the more intimate and detailed handling of the ninth and tenth books, with their wide range of interest and lack of dramatic concentration. Medina had too strong a feeling for design to relapse into a purely episodic treatment, but he came very near it in Book IX, and I think he was led to it, against the natural bent of his talent, by a desire to be faithful to his author.

The second point that is of great interest is the difficulty Medina found in representing Satan, and the means by which he tried to solve the problem. He is as aware as any modern critic of the progressive deterioration of Satan, and he portrays it by a striking, if crude, use of different conventional figures. In the first book he gives us the Archangel ruined; Satan not only has the form of an Archangel, he stands in the heroic pose of Michael beating down the dragon with his spear. The figure is brilliantly lit; the face is young, beautiful, and sorrowful. The only sign of his difference from the servants of God is in the long pointed ears that cling, satyr-like, to the sides of his head, and the two small horns that disfigure him. He is here the warrior angel 'that led th' imbattelld Seraphim to Warr' (I. 129). In the second book, where he is parleying with Sin and Death, this air of nobility has gone. His wings are less wide-spread, the pointed ears and horns are more noticeable; he looks older, and by his pose and expression recalls more a Restoration conception of a Roman general arguing with his opponents than a member of the heavenly host. The wings seem rather an irrelevant appendage to this military figure, not, as in the first picture, a symbol of celestial origin and power. This is Satan the politician. In the third plate Satan is alone; he has landed on the outer shell of the world after his perilous voyage, and Medina wishes somehow to show him as he is, not as he appears to his followers and allies, nor as he appears to his enemies, the human race. He seems to have felt that the archangelic type was unsuitable here, but that the popular representation of the devil was equally wrong; so he sought for a middle term and drew a figure that suggests to us a Greek satyr, a human figure with suggestions of the animal in the shaggy covering that shades the legs and thighs, and in the horns on its head. He is here the creature excluded from the realm of Grace, and has more of pathos than of horror about him. His next appearance is in Book IX, for in Lens's illustrations to Book IV he appears only in the shapes of cormorant and toad, and in Book VI he is indistinguishable from the other rebel angels. Here, at the moment of temptation, he is represented as the devil of popular imagination. He has the blackness of the Prince of Darkness, the great bat-wings, the goat-legs and feet, the horns and pointed ears. This is Satan the enemy of mankind. In Book X, on the other hand, where he is rejoicing at the meeting with Sin and Death, he has lost the distinctive appearance of the devil and is once more in the form of a satyr.

If it cannot be claimed that Medina succeeded in the almost impossible task of portraying Satan, all the same, his effort to follow Milton's mind is striking. He is aware of the deterioration of Satan as the poem proceeds, and displays it clearly, if crudely; but his awareness that Satan is in no sense the hero of the poem does not affect his recognition of the grandeur of the original presentation of him, as it has with some modern critics. He tries to give us both the tragic Satan and the wily tempter. But he feels a need of some bridge between the lost Archangel and the Devil 'with leer malign', and he finds this in the ambiguous figure of the satyr, which seems to have been the best equivalent he could find, among conventional artistic types, for Satan as he was, when active neither in war nor in temptation. Medina's difficulty in representing Satan makes us realize once more the originality and depth of Milton's creation, which no single type can represent. His unsuccessful but interesting attempt makes us ask ourselves how Milton himself wished us to envisage Satan when he started up 'discovered and surpriz'd' in his own likeness as 'the griesly King', and, unrecognized by the Celestial sentinels, 'pin'd his loss' on hearing the taunt of Zephon:

> Think not, revolted Spirit, thy shape the same,
> Or undiminisht brightness, to be known
> As when thou stoodst in Heav'n upright and pure.   (IV. 835–8.)

The next illustrators to *Paradise Lost*, Thornhill and Cheron, who provided head and tail pieces for Tonson's edition of 1720, abandoned the problem. Their Satan is unchanged from first to last, with no traces of his archangelic beauty. They portrayed a single degraded figure.[1]

Medina's illustrations continued to be reproduced, though in a more and more deplorable state, until 1784, and cannot have been without some influence, even though unconscious, on the imaginations of readers of the poem. Today they are unfamiliar and at first sight unimaginative. As works of art and interpretations of the poem they cannot compare with the illustrations of Blake, illuminated by profound spiritual conviction, or with those of Turner and Martin, whose imaginations responded to the Miltonic sublime and the Miltonic vague, and who rendered visually something of the stupendous Miltonic universe. But, pedestrian and literal as they are, their literalness would not, I believe, have displeased Milton, and to look at them gives us perhaps some indication of how *Paradise Lost* was read by men of its own century.[2]

[1] For a full discussion of the history of attempts to illustrate *Paradise Lost*, see C. H. Collins Baker, 'Some Illustrations of Milton's *Paradise Lost* (1688–1850)', *The Library*, Fifth Series, iii, 1948. I am much indebted to Mr. Collins Baker's article and to discussions with him before its appearance.

[2] Since this article was written, other writers have commented on illustrations of the expulsion scene. See K. Svendsen, 'John Martin and the Expulsion Scene in *Paradise Lost*', *Studies in English Literature, 1500–1900*, i (1961), 63–74, and Merritt Y. Hughes, 'Some Illustrators of Milton: the Expulsion from Paradise', *J.E.G.P.*, October 1961.

PRINTED IN GREAT BRITAIN
AT THE UNIVERSITY PRESS, OXFORD
BY VIVIAN RIDLER
PRINTER TO THE UNIVERSITY